AN INTRODUCTION TO

AIRBRUSHING

AND

P·H·O·T·O

RETOUCHING

BRETT BRECKON

AN INTRODUCTION TO
AIRBRUSHING
AND
P·H·O·T·O
RETOUCHING
BRETT BRECKON

Grange
BOOKS

A QUINTET BOOK

Published by Grange Books
An Imprint of Grange Books plc
The Grange
Grange Yard
London SE1 3AG

This edition published 1995

ISBN 1-85627-850-6

This book was designed and produced by
Quintet Publishing Limited
6 Blundell Street
London N7 9BH

Art Director: Peter Bridgewater
Designer: Ian Hunt
Editors: Chris Maynard, Judith Simons

Typeset in Great Britain by
Central Southern Typesetters, Eastbourne
Manufactured in Hong Kong by
Regent Publishing Services Limited
Printed in Singapore by
Star Standard Industries (Pte) Ltd.

The author and Quintet would like to extend special
thanks to Joanne Davies; Collins Publishing Limited;
Control Data Limited; Paul Jackson; Stephenson Moore
Limited; HTV Limited; Penknife Design Limited; Gomer
Press; Stills Design Group; Ken Warner and students of
the Falmouth School of Art and Design; Andy Penaluna
and students of the Faculty of Art and Design, West
Glamorgan Institute of Higher Education.

CONTENTS

I/N/T/R/O/D/U/C/T/I/O/N

The existence of this book reflects the way in which airbrushing has, in a few short years, exploded from obscurity to a high public profile. This fascinating art form has now become as accessible to hobbyists and students as it is to professionals. This book is designed to bridge the gap between beginners and professionals by breaking down a highly technical art form into small and comprehensible parts, each of which may be tackled at the reader's own pace.

Accessibility has also meant a great leap forward in the quality of airbrushing equipment available to the newcomer. By outlining the array of airbrushes and ancilliary equipment available, the first chapter describes how to build up your studio and equipment according to your needs. From there, each chapter marks a steady progression from your first tentative marks with an airbrush through to technical perfection.

Aside from its educational and instructional role, the book will also serve as a useful reference guide and source of inspiration years after you have completed its various exercises and projects.

LEFT: The Storm, *Brett Breckon. Airbrushing, no longer restricted to the domain of the chromium jukebox and plastic pinup, has grown and extended its boundaries to include such subjects as this, an illustration for a children's poem.*

RIGHT: The Claws of the Gryphon, *Brett Breckon. A combination of airbrushing techniques and media was used in this book jacket illustration to represent the contrasting textures of silk and gold. A simple vignette creates an atmospheric background.*

EQUIPMENT AND MATERIALS

A/I/R/B/R/U/S/H/E/S

Anybody who has spent time in a school art room will no doubt know what a mouth-diffuser is. Two short chromium-plated tubes, not much fatter than ballpoint pen refills, are hinged together in such a way that they can be separated at right angles. One of the tubes has a plastic mouthpiece, while the other tube is dipped into a container of ink or well-diluted paint. Blowing hard will cause ink to be drawn up the second tube and blown out of the diffuser, emerging as if by magic as a spray. The effect is always pleasing, and well worth the sore cheeks and moments of breathlessness.

The airbrush is no more than a development of a very basic principle which dictates that air forced at high pressure over a hollow tube causes liquid to be drawn up from a reservoir where the air pressure is lower. Similarly, an air supply channelled through to the nozzle of an airbrush, on meeting a supply of paint (usually transported along a needle) causes that paint to be atomized and forced out of the airbrush nozzle in a fine, controllable spray — just how fine and how controllable depends upon the airbrush.

It is important to identify very early on the sort of work you hope to produce, and to look at how that work can best be achieved. You will have to choose from many types of airbrush. When starting out, there is a tendency to think more about the cost than the capabilities

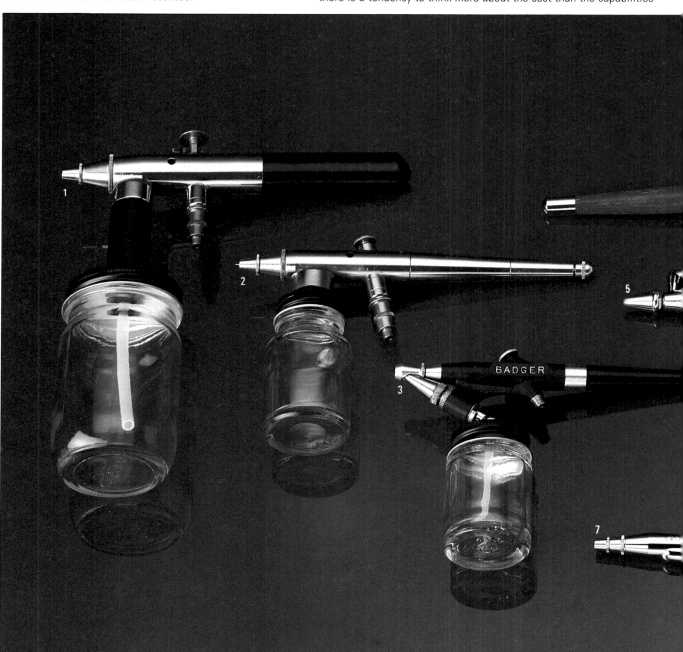

of the equipment, but try to resist this, especially if your aims are to progress to the finer points of detailed graphic work.

The first thing you need to know is that there are two main categories of airbrush; single-action models where you control only the air supply, and double-action models where you have simultaneous control over the air and the paint supply. With both types the control is a trigger situated on top of the airbrush body which you operate with your index finger while holding the instrument like a pen. The following breakdown of various types of airbrush will help you to understand how they work and what their limitations are, and so help you make the all-important decision about which airbrush to acquire first.

BELOW: *The wide selection of airbrushes now produced can be confusing, if not bewildering. The following selection of models illustrates the available range of basic types.*
1 *Large capacity, suction-feed, double-action airbrush. Thayer and Chandler model C.*
2 *Single-action, suction-feed airbrush. Thayer and Chandler model E.*
3 *Single-action, external-mix with suction-feed. Badger 350.*
4 *The 'thoroughbred' of airbrushes, the* turbo. Paasche AB Turbo.
5 *Double-action, internal-mix, suction-feed airbrush with side cup. Paasche VJR.*
6 *Double-action model with fitted bowl. DeVilbiss Super 63.*
7 *Double-action with small colour compartment. Olympos HP 100.*
8 *Spray gun. DeVilbiss MB.*
9 *Fixed double-action. Conopois F.*

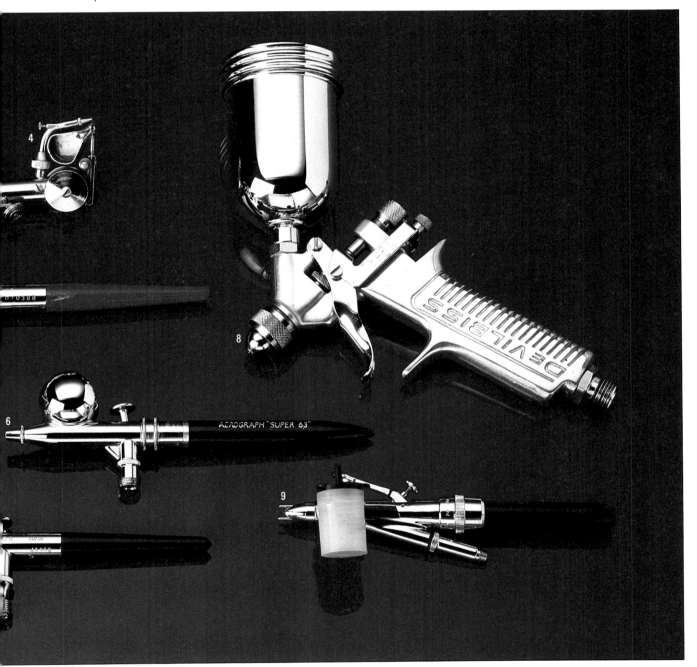

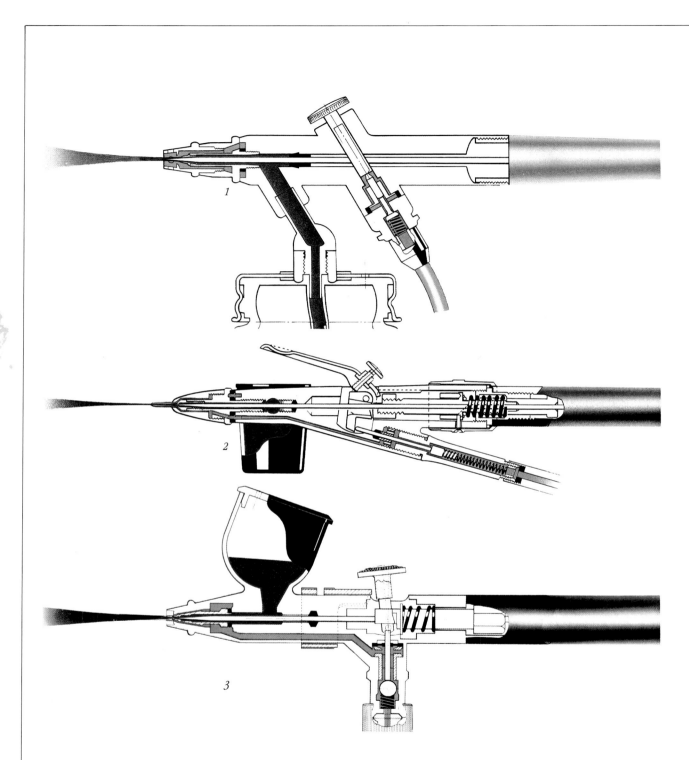

ABOVE: Airbrush design. *There are three main categories of airbrush used for precise and detailed work. They are all internal-mix, but vary in the degree of control, over the mix of paint and air, offered to the artist.*

1 *Single-action models work to a preset ratio of paint and air.*

2 *Double-action fixed models are also preset, but are more flexible to work with.*

3 *Independent double-action airbrushes allow constant variation of paint to air flow.*

SINGLE-ACTION AIRBRUSHES

EXTERNAL-MIX

This really is the very simplest of airbrushes. It is not much more advanced than a mouth-diffuser, although it allows for a small amount of control by adjustments to the front-mounted nozzle. This has to be preset by experimenting beforehand and, for a while at least, a fairly well balanced spray pattern can be achieved. Inevitably, it drifts back out of tune and needs to be reset.

You should not be deceived into thinking that this 'cheap and cheerful' tool will make a good starting point for an airbrushing career. Its use is strictly limited to laying large flat areas of colour, or at most using very basic masking techniques. External-mix airbrushes are usually known as 'hobbyist' tools and they are best used to apply colours to models, backgrounds, posters and the like.

EXTERNAL-MIX WITH NEEDLE

This is the next step up the airbrush scale. Here the paint is transported to the nozzle along a needle for a more controlled flow. Again, much pre-setting and experimentation needs to be carried out before you start spraying onto your finished artwork if you want to get the best from this kind of instrument. However, the drawbacks of all external-mix airbrushes will still be encountered, most notably the lack of a really fine spray pattern.

INTERNAL-MIX

Now we are getting closer to the type of instrument that can achieve the spectacular finishes most of you taking up airbrushing would wish for. With an internal-mix airbrush the paint and air meet within the nozzle to give a fine and even spray without the spatter and inconsistencies of external-mix. The flow of compressed air is channelled around the nozzle, through which a centralized needle runs, carrying the paint to its tip. This rush of high pressure draws the paint out by creating a partial vacuum between itself and the lower pressure in the paint reservoir. By altering the setting of the needle, the width of the spray pattern emerging from the front of the airbrush is varied. Again this needs to be done before you start spraying as the setting cannot be changed in mid-flow. With regular use it is possible to become quite adept at spraying and altering as you work, thus getting good results with a range of spray patterns.

However, a single-action, internal-mix airbrush is still a very limiting tool if the best airbrushing techniques are required.

DOUBLE-ACTION AIRBRUSHES

If your airbrushing ambitions lie *anywhere* beyond the simple ability to lay down a flat colour or a graded background, then at some point you will probably need a double-action airbrush. This versatile tool makes all the more basic models pale into insignificance, and by mastering it you have at your fingertips the capacity to produce all the finishes and effects that have given airbrush illustration that special magic. This certainly is the type of airbrush that the professional illustrator and retoucher would choose, and if you wish to explore airbrushing in any depth, it is the type that you would do best to master.

In the double-action airbrush you can control air and paint flow with just your index finger on the trigger. Air is released as you press down, and then paint flows out as you draw back on the trigger – the farther you draw back the more paint you release. A good double-action airbrush will thus give you a range of spray patterns from a

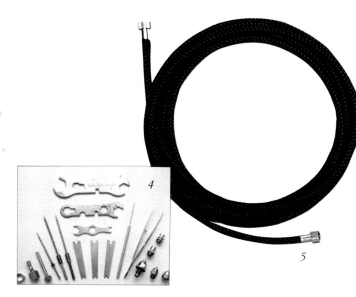

ABOVE: *Some airbrush designs allow for removable colours cups 1 and jars 2. An airbrush holder 3 is essential.*

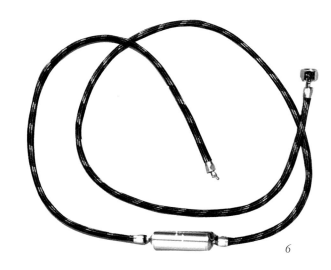

ABOVE: *Many airbrushes have special tools 4 for dismantling and cleaning operations. It is advisable to keep spare needles and nozzle assemblies. A good length of air hose 5 and 6 is necessary, but make sure it is compatible with your make of airbrush.*

pencil line to a 2-in (5-cm) fan. If you do decide on a double-action airbrush there are two types to choose from.

INDEPENDENT DOUBLE-ACTION

This is the tool that most professionals opt for. Mastering its flexibility so that freehand work can be tackled with confidence takes a little time. Some people learn more quickly than others, but in the end it is only a matter of co-ordination and quite soon you forget to think about the tool as it becomes merely an extension of your hand while you work, with your forefinger moving the trigger backward and forward unconsciously, leaving your eye and brain free to concentrate on the image you are creating. With the independent double-action models the full range of trigger movement is available at all times, so that while spraying, the paint flow can be adjusted or stopped altogether. Some models have a tubular cam by the trigger with which you can preset the width of spray without the danger of letting too much paint out.

FIXED DOUBLE-ACTION

There are a small number of fixed double-action airbrushes available. These are easier to operate than the independent double-action models since the trigger, although still controlling both the air and paint, does so to a fixed and preset ratio. These models need less dexterity than the independent types, while being capable of equally fine work. For that reason they make good general studio brushes, being capable, with a little extra patience, of quality work with less emphasis on expertise.

R/E/S/E/R/V/O/I/R/S

All airbrushes have some sort of container to hold a supply of the medium being fed through them. Various manufacturers provide a wide range of shapes, sizes, designs and positions of these on their airbrushes.

There are two methods by which paint can be fed into the airstream, suction-feed or gravity-feed.

SUCTION-FEED

With suction-feed there is a reservoir below the body of the airbrush, either a glass jar or a metal cup, from which paint is drawn up. The same principle which makes a diffuser work, that is, a higher air pressure flowing above, creating a pressure drop below, forces paint upward into the nozzle assembly. The advantages of the suction-feed type are that more paint can be held in the usually larger jar, and that the reservoir can quickly and easily be removed and changed. The biggest disadvantages are that these larger jars not only get in the way for close, finely detailed work, but they also make the airbrush unbalanced and ungainly.

GRAVITY-FEED

With gravity-feed airbrushes the reservoir is either on top or to one side of the pen, and gravity aids the flow of paint to the nozzle. On many of these models the reservoir forms a permanent part of the tool, being either a cup rising up out of the main body, or merely a recess in the body itself. This creates the only drawback, a limited liquid capacity. However, there are gravity-feed airbrushes with

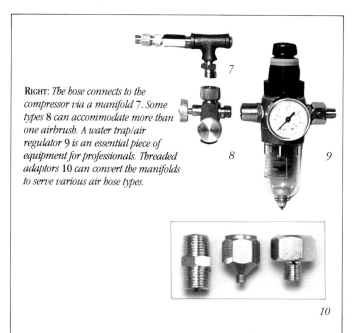

RIGHT: *The hose connects to the compressor via a manifold 7. Some types 8 can accommodate more than one airbrush. A water trap/air regulator 9 is an essential piece of equipment for professionals. Threaded adaptors 10 can convert the manifolds to serve various air hose types.*

BELOW: *An air can 11, of the type manufactured for airbrushing, can be useful to the beginner, or in case of emergency.*

A/I/R S/U/P/P/L/I/E/S

Perhaps the biggest shock awaiting any would-be airbrush artist is the cost of setting up with all the right equipment, and this includes a good supply of compressed air. Having just paid a fair amount for an airbrush it is heartbreaking to find that it does not live up to expectations and seems incapable of achieving all that the manufacturer promised. But this can happen, especially if you try to work with an inadequate air supply. Deciding on the right supply for your airbrush involves looking at the options available, and choosing the one best suited to your financial and physical situation.

CONTAINERIZED AIR

THE CAR TYRE
The cheapest form of compressed air is a car tyre. Though not the most attractive object to bring into your studio, an old car tyre still on its rim will none the less provide a rudimentary supply of air for your airbrush, which you can keep topped up to a workable pressure by using a foot pump. Do not, however, expect miracles from your airbrush.

THE AIR CAN
Many newcomers to airbrushing undertake their earliest exercises and projects with a pre-packaged successor to the car tyre, the compressed air can. Similar to aerosol cans, though minus the spraying head, they are produced by airbrush manufacturers and others specially for this end of the market. They have a threaded attaching point at the top to which a control valve is attached to provide a link with the air hose, leaving you ready to spray cleanly and noiselessly. Their drawbacks are a short life span and a slowly weakening pressure as they empty. There is no harm in starting with air cans, but most who do usually decide quite quickly that a more permanent investment will, in the long run, provide cheaper compressed air. They keep an air can purely for emergencies.

CARBON DIOXIDE CYLINDERS
CO_2 cylinders are yet another kind of containerized air supply. These can be either bought or hired, although if you adopt this method of powering your airbrush you will need to be sure of a good local supplier for refills. You will also need an outlet attachment with a built-in regulator and measuring gauge to avoid running out of air half way through a job. These cylinders are a step up from air cans, being longer lasting and more controllable, but they also lose their pressure eventually and run out; an inconvenience that the serious user can best do without.

COMPRESSORS

Undoubtedly the best and, in the long run, most economical air supply is provided by a compressor. Thanks to consumer demand, there is a vast array of models and types to choose from, ranging from the cheap 'adequate-but-basic' models to the smoothly versatile 'perfection-at-a-price' types.

THE STORAGE COMPRESSOR
Ideally, you will want something that gives you moisture-free air, in a constant flow at a variable but controlled pressure. The simplest way to achieve this ideal is to buy the best, which is a storage

removable reservoirs, and these are quite often of a larger capacity than the 5cc or so of the cup type, and only 1cc of the recessed well type. By and large, though, this limited capacity is not a genuine problem, once you get used to seeing how far a small amount of your medium will go. Many users put up with constantly having to fill their reservoirs for the pleasure of working with these slim, well-balanced precision airbrushes.

compressor. This is an electrically driven motor that compresses air by means of a piston forcing the air in its cylinder, through a valve system and into a storage tank, until the desired preset pressure has built up. At this point the motor automatically cuts out. The air is drawn from this storage tank through a connecting hose, past a water trap, to the airbrush, which receives a supply of non-pulsing and moisture-free air at the desired pressure. A switch operates to restart the compressor when the pressure in the tank drops below a certain level. The only thing you have to do is reset the pressure should your needs change.

THE DIRECT COMPRESSOR

If this type of compressor is out of your reach, a cheaper, less sophisticated set-up is a direct compressor. This has an electric motor generating compressed air, either with a small piston or a rubber diaphragm, feeding directly to the airbrush. There is no storage thank. There are four problems encountered here. Firstly, these small compressors tend to be noisy, and since there is no storage tank they run constantly while you use air. Secondly, because the air hose is connected directly to the pump, a rapid 'pulsing' flow travels to the airbrush, and this can be seen in the lines of colour you produce if you are moving the airbrush quickly. Thirdly, the air has all the moisture created by the compressing action still in it, and this moisture will build up into water droplets, which will splatter out of the airbrush onto your artwork. Finally, the pressure created by these compressors is determined by the manufacturer and is not controlled directly.

Despite all these drawbacks, a direct compressor makes a very adequate source of air for many people, and there are steps you can take to improve the quality and quantity of the air it produces. The problem of pulsing is, for a start, fractionally less obvious in the diaphragm type of compressor, which also tends to run quieter. Using a foot switch to turn the motor on and off dispenses with having to return constantly to the electric switch, thus keeping the running time to a minimum. But by far the best improvement to these smaller compressors is the addition of a moisture trap/air regulator. This allows you to regulate the pressure travelling to your airbrush, thus giving you the full range of effects available, while drawing out the moisture from the air, catching it in a glass bowl below which is a small release valve for easy drainage.

SETTING THE AIR PRESSURE

When you have decided upon the air source of your choice, and if this lets you regulate pressure, then you will need to set a working pressure for your airbrush. A good starting point is 30 psi (pounds per square inch), which may also read on some gauges as '2 bar'. This is a standard pressure for airbrushing, the one most often set

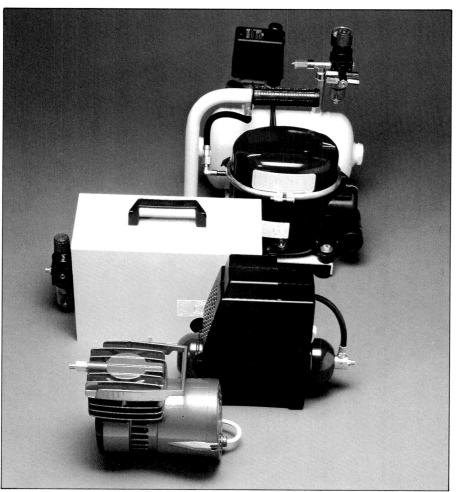

LEFT: *The four types of compressor shown here illustrate the range available. (From front to back) The basic diaphragm direct compressor, if fitted with a water trap and air regulator, is adequate for the beginner, if noisy. The more advanced, manual compressor has a small storage tank that will eliminate the 'pulsing' problem inherent in the basic model. The more sophisticated manual compressor has a quieter motor and a built-in air filter and regulator, while the fully automatic compressor, at the rear, provides a perfect air supply for up to four airbrushes.*

for general use. As you become more proficient you will want to experiment with different pressures. You will find that decreasing the pressure has the same effect as thickening the paint, producing a coarser-grained spray or even a spatter if you let the pressure drop right down. At the other end of the scale it is not wise to work above a maximum of 40 psi (2.6 bar).

A/C/C/E/S/S/O/R/I/E/S

Once you have your airbrush and compressor, preferably with moisture trap and air regulator, the only other necessity is an air hose to connect the two together. However, there are a few accessories worth listing which, although not absolutely essential to begin with, will need explanation here so that you are aware of them for future reference.

AIR HOSES

You must be sure to get the correct air hose for your airbrush since all manufacturers have their own design, with its own threaded coupling. The right one will fit directly onto your airbrush, but a thread adaptor may have to go onto your compressor to make the connection at that end. Checking with your supplier will help to clarify this. Also make sure to get an air hose long enough to reach from the compressor to your drawing board, with plenty of surplus for freedom of movement. Route it in such a way that it will avoid being crushed by feet or chair legs.

NOZZLE SETS

When you buy your first airbrush, check what is available from manufacturers as accessories to their products. You will not necessarily buy everything they have to offer, but putting yourself in the picture may help to solve technical problems later. Some companies, for example, produce different nozzle sets for their airbrushes, to help cope with everything from large-area coverage to fine-line spraying. One British company provides a useful gadget, the spatter cap, which when attached in place of the nozzle produces a spatter effect that is a great asset when illustrating a textured surface like gravel, or granite. With all other types of airbrush this effect has to be created by experimenting with low air pressures, and clever manipulation of the trigger control.

AIRBRUSH NEEDLES

Airbrush needles are very delicate pieces of equipment. Careful maintenance and patient cleaning will help prolong the life of each needle, but severe damage, especially to the needle tip, spells the end of one needle and the need for an immediate replacement. It is a good idea to have spare needles available at all times.

COLOUR CUPS

Some airbrushes that have removable colour cups or jars can be fitted with different sized interchangeable units to accommodate different jobs. It is a good idea to carry spares, especially if you only need a small amount of colour, because reducing the weight and bulk of your airbrush by changing to a smaller cup will make fine

work easier. Also, a readily available colour cup filled with water or solvent to blow through the airbrush quickly will prevent colour drying up on the needle and nozzle if you have to leave the work for a short time, say to answer the telephone.

AIRBRUSH HOLDERS

Having an airbrush holder clamped to your desk edge will certainly save you the heartache caused by a dropped or knocked over airbrush. Holders are available commercially, but the more practical airbrush user will create an ingenious cradle from a metal coat-hanger, or even a couple of plastic cup-hooks. But whatever is used, the airbrush must sit horizontally and safely in it to avoid any spills or knocks.

S/P/E/C/I/A/L/I/Z/E/D E/Q/U/I/P/M/E/N/T

When you have mastered the basics of airbrushing, there will hopefully be a plethora of exciting challenges ahead. With each one you will learn more about airbrush art and about your abilities, and you may decide to invest in more equipment to increase the scope of your work. Here are three pieces of equipment that you may consider when this stage is reached but which for the beginner may be a little too specialized.

THE SPRAY GUN

This is a smaller version of the industrial sprayers used in the car industry and elsewhere, and is a useful tool for laying down large flat areas of colour for backgrounds, or for use on murals, or large three-dimensional pieces. It is gravity-fed from a very large cup on top of its short body, and works with a fluid needle adjusted at the rear in the same way as a single-action airbrush.

THE TURBO AIRBRUSH

The true thoroughbred of the airbrush world is the complex and expensive turbo. It is the most precise airbrush available, capable of producing the very finest of hairlines, but is also the most difficult and demanding instrument to master. Just by looking at it you will know that it is a very strange animal, and it does indeed have characteristics that are all its own. The most obvious of these is the turbine from which it gets its name. This is propelled by the airflow, accelerating up to 20,000 rpm (revolutions per minute), and drives the front-mounted fluid needle back and forth, at equally high speeds, at right angles to the airbrush body. Another jet of air meets the needle and blows across it, taking the small amount of paint that the needle collects from the colour cup on each movement. To add to this complexity, the very nature of the design means that the spray produced is not in line with the airbrush body, but offset to one side. This is perhaps the aspect of this unique airbrush hardest to master.

THE AIR ERASER

One method of achieving highlights in airbrush illustration is to remove already applied paint to leave the white surface showing

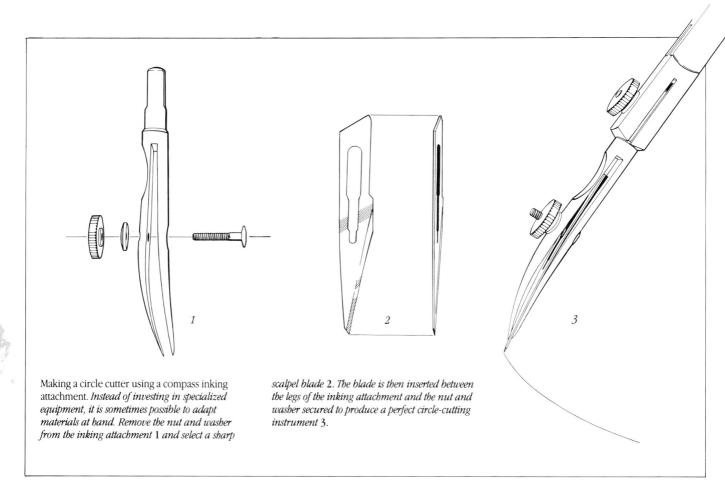

Making a circle cutter using a compass inking attachment. *Instead of investing in specialized equipment, it is sometimes possible to adapt materials at hand. Remove the nut and washer from the inking attachment* 1 *and select a sharp*

scalpel blade 2. *The blade is then inserted between the legs of the inking attachment and the nut and washer secured to produce a perfect circle-cutting instrument* 3.

through. This can be done by scratching with a sharp tool, or rubbing with an eraser. Both of these methods are a little crude and can damage paint around the area being removed. An air eraser, on the other hand, does a much finer job, and since its qualities are similar to that of the airbrush, the finish it achieves is much more sympathetic to the artwork. In simple terms the air eraser works like a sandblaster, but uses a very fine pumice powder in the airstream to erode the paint surface.

Y/O/U/R S/T/U/D/I/O

Whatever kind of work has brought you to the airbrush, you will need a studio space that is conducive to the nature of airbrushing. A reasonably large room is preferable, since under heavy usage an airbrush puts a lot of atomized paint into the atmosphere and this is unhealthy in a confined space. Good ventilation is a must for the same reason.

Natural light is the best for all kinds of painting, and colour work in particular suffers under artificial light conditions. Obviously, it is not possible always to have an ideal north-facing window for light consistency. If you do not, you should try to position your work surface so that you do not work in harsh direct sunlight, since the strong shadows cast by blinds, window frames, even dirty or imperfect glass, will make it difficult to concentrate on the finish you are achieving with the airbrush. Inevitably, you will have to work under electric lights, too, and you should organize a system to suit yourself.

For example, strip lighting is good for general illumination with angled lamps above your board for close work. Try not to allow the room to become too warm, as this will increase the humidity and also affect some materials. Masking film has a tendency to blister and lift from artwork surfaces if it becomes too warm, and this can be caused by body heat and close lamps as well as by general room temperature. This is doubly frustrating since not only will the mask lift off when spraying, but the adhesive backing also becomes more tacky. On cooling down again, it sticks more persistently than it should, which can damage your painting.

Your work surface can be flat or sloping, and should be apart from the area that you do your drawing in, especially technical drawing as that needs greater cleanliness. Ultimately, your studio will design itself through constant use and experiment. All you can plan for at the outset is your personal comfort. By being comfortable you will have greater patience for your work.

STUDIO EQUIPMENT

Listing every item of studio equipment that might be useful to all airbrush artists is quite impossible. No apology is therefore made for the following list which is culled from a studio doing mostly two-dimensional illustration and photo-retouching.

Drawing equipment is indispensable in any studio, and beautifully sharpened pencils the most important. To wield these properly, there should be set squares, rulers, French curves, and ellipse templates always to hand, as well as hard and soft erasers. Cutting tools to prepare masks should include scalpels, and those with the more slender handles are preferable since they are easier to use when cutting tricky shapes. Similarly, longer, thinner blades work better and obscure the lines you are cutting far less. A heavy-duty studio knife is better for slicing thick boards, and a steel cutting edge is safer than using a plastic ruler as a cutting guide. Compasses with a cutting attachment will also prove useful.

You will find that fine sable paintbrushes will be needed to finish off details on your artwork, while larger and coarser brushes are useful for mixing paint, transferring it to your airbrush, and then cleaning out the colour cup afterward. The palette, used for mixing paint, ought to have small but fairly deep wells, and should be kept scrupulously clean between jobs. Jars filled with plenty of clean water always need to be at hand, because the care and maintenance of your airbrush is paramount, and constant cleaning is essential.

Add to these items supplies of adhesive tape, rolls of tissue paper, cotton wool buds for cleaning operations, lighter fluid (cleaning solvent) to remove grease, and a soft dusting brush to remove particles from your artwork, and the basic list is almost complete. This list will almost certainly be added to through experience and individual need, and your studio workspace will soon take on a life all of its own.

MAKING A CIRCLE-CUTTER USING A COMPASS INKING ATTACHMENT

Rather than buying a special circle-cutting attachment for your compass it is possible to create your own, provided your compass kit has an inking pen, as shown in the diagrams here.

Remove the adjusting nut and washer, and withdraw the small bolt. It is now possible to slide a cutting blade between the legs of the inking attachment. This can be secured by replacing the small bolt, letting its shaft slide through the fixing slot in the blade. The nut

should be tightened enough to hold the blade in place while cutting your circle.

Do not tighten it right up as this could strain the natural springing action of the inking attachment.

G/R/O/U/N/D/S A/N/D M/E/D/I/A

The ground is the surface upon which you work. Depending on your aims this may have two or three dimensions, and be composed of virtually any material. What you have to do is balance a chosen ground with a suitable medium that will adhere to and cover it. Some of you will perhaps be using an airbrush on three-dimensional modelling projects, or maybe for work on fabrics, or some other surfaces that require specialized materials. This book cannot possibly hope to cover all these needs, but common sense and consultation with your materials' supplier will go a long way to explain compatible grounds and media for your work. Here are some of the more common grounds and media used in airbrush work.

BOARDS AND PAPERS

For the illustrator the ideal ground is flat, smooth, hard and very white. Fine line art boards usually fulfil these needs perfectly and there are several makes available from most graphic supply stockists. Composed of a strong, thick surface paper, dry-mounted to a supporting board with a pre-stressed backing to maintain flatness, they provide a ground that is tough enough to withstand scraping or erasing, yet will not discolour or react chemically with the applied medium.

Bristol board is an alternative favoured by many illustrators because the softer surface finish also lends itself to brush and wash

RIGHT: There are many brands and types of ground suitable for various types of airbrush work. Hot Pressed art boards are very popular with all illustrators, as are watercolour and Bristol boards, and choice depends on the requirements of the artist and the medium used. Acetate makes a useful ground for the animator or technical illustrator.

Lighter fluid (cleaning solvent) is indispensable for cleaning equipment and for degreasing boards before commencing work.

A variety of erasers are always necessary. Stick erasers are made from a hard, gritty compound and are used if pigment is to be completely removed, for example, in the addition of highlights. Softer compound and putty erasers are useful for more delicate cleaning-up operations.

applications which may be used together with airbrushing. However, for pure airbrush work with much use of masking film this surface will prove too soft and liable to 'plucking' (where fibres in the board loosen and lift away), leaving white marks in previously sprayed areas.

Watercolour papers and boards have a textured surface which will be picked out and exaggerated when paint is airbrushed across them. This can be used to positive effect if your prefer a free approach to paint application and masking. But these papers are relatively soft and fibrous and will suffer from 'plucking' when adhesive masking films are used.

If an illustration is to be used in montage, or if it must be flexible enough to be wrapped around the drum of a scanning machine for four-colour reproduction, it may be necessary to work on paper.

STRETCHING ART (HOT-PRESSED) PAPER

If that work also involves a lot of masking or the heavy use of colour then the best surface to work on will probably be a fine line art paper. Such papers are available in pads or in single large sheets, but they need to be stretched so that they stay flat as they dry. The guidelines below will help you to achieve perfection each and every time.

1 Place your paper, drawing surface down, onto the board. (One of the advantages of working on this paper, which is fairly thin, is that drawings can be traced, using a lightbox, directly onto the sheet before it is stretched, provided minor distortions caused by stretching are acceptable.) Soak the sponge or cloth in water and squeeze out, then coat the back of the paper evenly and quickly.

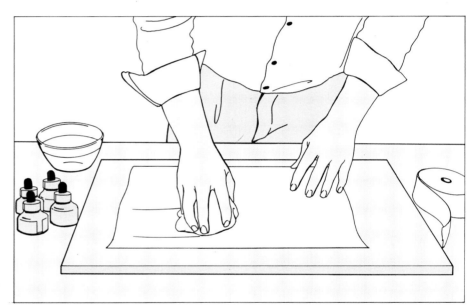

2 The paper will react immediately and start to roll up – be prepared for this and work quickly. Turn the paper over, drawing side *up*, and hold it down at the four corners with paperweights. Take a length of gummed strip, several inches longer than the longest edge of the paper, wet the gum and lower the tape carefully to position it along one long edge of the paper, about ½ in (1 cm) in. The rest of its width will be pressed firmly to the board. You can now remove the two weights nearest the tape.

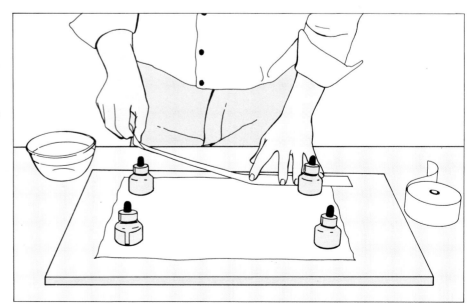

MATERIALS
A sheet of fine line art (Hot Pressed) paper.
A *clean*, flat, wooden drawing board, with no remnants of loose colour or previous stretching tape. This has to be larger than your paper.
2 in (5 cm) wide gummed strip.
Four clean, dry paperweights or other heavy objects.
Clean water.
Small sponge or clean cloth.

Recently, manufacturers have taken note of how awkward this process can be and now produce stripper-board, which has an impermanently mounted fine line surface paper that can be peeled away once the illustration is complete and ready for scanning, and then returned to the backing board for safe storage.

Whichever surface you choose to work on, there is one golden rule to observe, and that is cleanliness. You should always avoid allowing fingers to touch the board as this will allow natural skin oils to be transferred onto the surface which will show up when paint is applied. Lighter fluid (cleaning solvent) applied to cotton wool, or soft tissue wiped evenly across a fine line surface before commencing work is a good precaution against greasy marks.

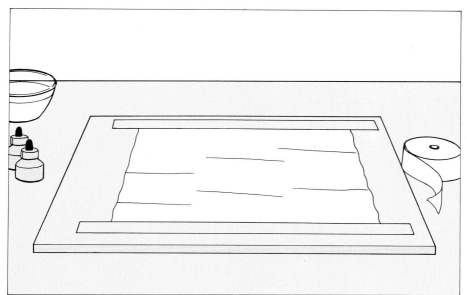

3 Turn the board around so that the second long edge of the paper is near you, and prepare to tape this edge down. Gently pull the paper flat holding the two free corners to reduce as much as possible the cockling that will have built up, but do not try, or expect, to pull it taut. Place the second wetted strip down to anchor the second long edge. At all times avoid letting water drops fall onto the drawing surface of the paper as marks will show through later airbrushing. Remove the last two retaining weights.

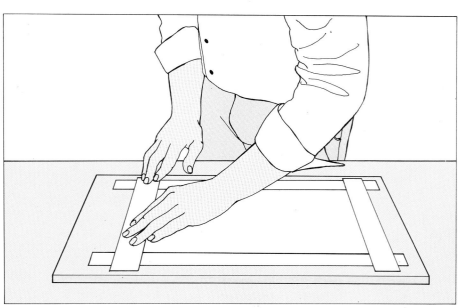

4 The two shorter sides can now be taped down. Avoid the temptation to press any cockling flat – the paper will flatten out naturally on drying. Allow the paper to dry out naturally, away from a direct or concentrated heat source, otherwise uneven drying will occur, pulling at the sheet and causing ribs to form.

A WORD OF CAUTION – when spraying onto stretched paper avoid over-wetting the surface since this can cause cockling. Although the paper will dry flat again, cockling leads to difficulty with masking and to uneven tones on drying.

MEDIA

Almost any medium that can be diluted to the consistency of milk can be fed through an airbrush, but before you begin, some consideration has to be given to the tool itself. It is essential that whatever liquid is put through an airbrush can be thoroughly ejected afterward, and so prior thought about suitable solvents and cleaners will save the heartache of expensive repairs. Rigorous and regular cleaning cannot be emphasized enough if you are to get the best from your airbrush.

GOUACHE

The most common media used in airbrushing are water-based, and of these gouache is especially popular with many artists, largely because of its strong colour and opacity. Care has to be taken when mixing gouache to find the right consistency. Certain colours pose a problem as the coarseness and density of their compounds causes them to separate out in the dilutant in the palette. However, perseverance with this versatile medium can produce the finest results of all from airbrushing.

WATERCOLOUR

Artists' quality watercolours, as opposed to the cheaper and inferior amateur watercolours, are another ideal medium and are available in tube form. Working with this translucent paint necessitates perhaps a greater degree of patience than with gouache in order to build up tones, but the careful application of fine layers can produce very dramatic effects that are hard to beat. Often gouache and watercolour are used together on the same painting so as to get the best of both worlds – opacity and translucence, strong colour and fine tone.

Watercolours are also available in liquid form, developed specially for use in airbrushes and resemble inks in their consistency and make-up. Bright, vivid colours are their trademark, and as they come ready mixed they are a favourite medium for beginners.

INKS

Drawing inks, too, can be used, and again are available in ranges developed for airbrush use. They often come in bottles with a handy pipette dropper in the cap which not only makes it easy to fill the colour cup, but also to mix colours exactly, drop by drop. When using inks, care must be taken not to allow them to dry inside the airbrush, since on drying they become waterproof and quite hard – and a major chore to remove.

Some media are best left alone during your earliest days of airbrushing (their natures and drying habits only make it harder to learn the techniques of the art). By all means experiment later, but to begin with, walk before you run.

ACRYLIC AND TEMPERA

Acrylic and tempera are two water-soluble paints that dry water-resistant, whose qualities you may like to use in your airbrush work. There is no reason not to, but great care and attention are required in their application, especially acrylics which dry to a tough plastic skin. Clean the airbrush carefully after use.

LACQUER, ENAMEL AND OIL PAINTS

Lacquer, enamel and oil-based paints are also to be treated carefully. Some of the solvents necessary to flush them out can be damaging to the non-metallic parts of the airbrush, such as the vital rubber 'o'-ring that seals the nozzle.

FIXATIVES

If you work with a medium such as gouache, which powders slightly when dry and gets lifted in small quantities by protective paper or film, it is usually advisable to apply a fixative to consolidate the pigment. There are various brands of aerosol fixative on the market which perform the task adequately, although they should be tested thoroughly on the paint you are using before you commit yourself to covering a valuable piece of artwork with any one of them.

The major drawback with these types of fixative is that being alcohol-based they are alien to gouache. Later additional work may be difficult or impossible if a heavy coating has been given to a painting. A far more satisfactory fixing medium, therefore, is gum arabic solution, a mixture of two parts water to one part gum arabic

RIGHT: *Gouache is a favourite medium with many airbrush artists, and it produces a perfect opaque covering. Most commonly available in tube form, the highest quality brands are recommended as the pigment is more finely ground.*

P A R R O T S by Ean Taylor

*This is an example of how the subject matter can
suggest the appropriate medium. Here the artist has
used the transparent brilliance provided by ink to
portray the bright, vivid plumage of the birds.*

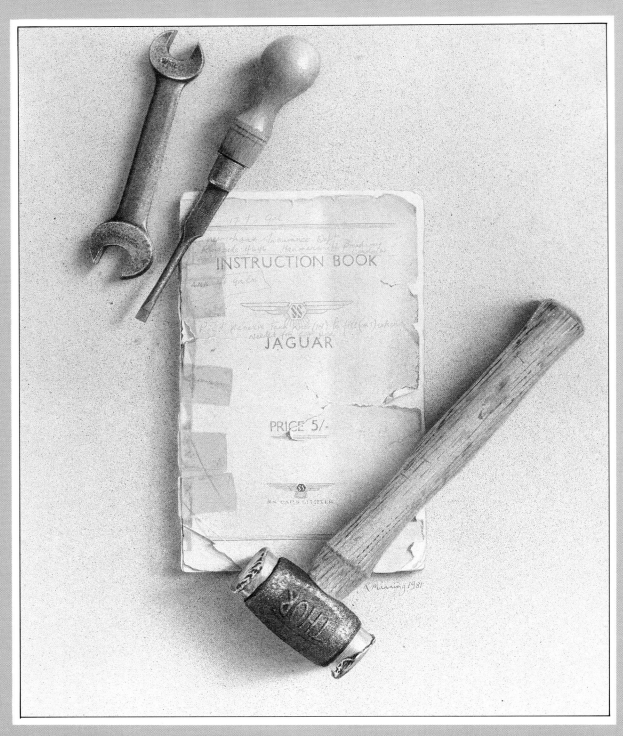

ABOVE: *The artist, Richard Manning, has exploited the delicate nature of watercolour to achieve this faded, almost photographic effect. A spatter cap was used to create the textured background and fine brushwork was added to detail the wooden handle.*

which can be sprayed through your airbrush. Since both ingredients are indigenous to gouache themselves, they are harmless to the colours; you can even work over the top of gum arabic if the need arises. Indeed, you may occasionally find it wise to fix part of a painting that has a soft and delicate surface before moving on to complete the work.

As a word of caution, when you have sprayed gum arabic solution through your airbrush, always flush it out completely and quickly to prevent a thin, invisible film of gum from drying on the needle and nozzle, which will seriously hinder it working properly.

Waterproof colours, such as inks, are unlikely to require any fixative. Likewise, with oil paint and acrylic, although there are varnishes and acrylic media available, both in bottles and in aerosol cans, which can be used as fixatives.

For all pieces of work it is advisable to cover the finished surface with a sheet of clear acetate taped firmly to the board edge. This will protect the artwork from fingerprints, scratches, and the attentions of any unwelcome foreign bodies which may harm it.

M/A/S/K/I/N/G

Masking is the method by which the paint spray is confined to one area of a drawing at any one time. A mask provides a solid barrier to paint overspray while also giving an accurate outline of the image being coloured. Making an accurate and precise mask is essential to all good airbrush art. A sound knowledge of what type of masking to use and for what effect will improve your work enormously. There are two general masking techniques, these being 'fixed' and 'loose' masking.

FIXED FILM MASKING

Fixed masking creates a hard-edged image, and is the mainstay of most airbrush artists' techniques. The commonest material used is a transparent, low-tack adhesive film, which comes in sheet form or

on rolls. A piece of this is cut large enough to cover your drawing, and is peeled from its backing paper and smoothed down into place. The area to be sprayed is then cut out with a sharp scalpel. This area of film is then lifted away from the drawing, exposing the bare board below, onto which you spray. Experience will tell you that only very light pressure on the scalpel is needed to pierce the film without cutting the board; making sure that your scalpel blade is always sharp will help it glide around even tight little corners. Experience will also show you not to flood the area with paint as this will cause bleeding, with excess wet paint seeping under the edge of the mask.

When you have finished work on one area, and it has been allowed to dry thoroughly, it can be covered up and a new area exposed for spraying. It is possible, with some types of work, to cut all the areas to be sprayed at the same time, but only uncover the surface to be worked on a piece at a time, replacing each piece of film carefully and accurately before moving on to another area. However, while this may be time-saving as far as cutting is concerned, there are two major drawbacks. Firstly, the film becomes covered in colour, obscuring areas sprayed earlier and making colour matching a matter of memory. Secondly, the film does stretch, which means that large or complicated shapes can be difficult to replace exactly. A much more practical solution for protecting an illustrated surface is to cut a window a little larger than the area to be coloured from a sheet of clean paper, which will cover the rest of the drawing. Apply masking film across this window to the board below and work through the window until the area inside it is completed. As you work through the exercises in this book you will soon learn more about the techniques of fixed film masking.

LIQUID MASKING

Liquid masking is a form of fixed mask which was very common in the days before the manufacture of masking film, but which nowadays is used much more rarely. Liquid mask is a rubber compound which can be applied finely by brush and then allowed to dry before being sprayed over. A soft eraser will lift it off the board with gentle rubbing.

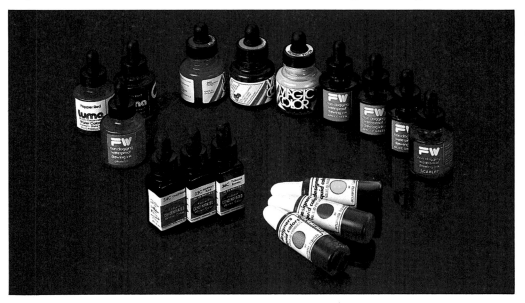

LEFT: *Inks and liquid watercolours are popular with airbrush artists because they are available ready-mixed for easy application and in a bright range of colours. When using inks, attention to cleaning becomes more critical as they become waterproof on drying. It is essential, therefore, to purchase the appropriate solution – check with your supplier if in doubt.*

1 *These step-by-step illustrations for a concept car help to explain some of the techniques used in masking. Firstly, using fixed film masking, the black recess and the chromium hub and rim are sprayed.*

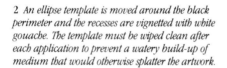

2 *An ellipse template is moved around the black perimeter and the recesses are vignetted with white gouache. The template must be wiped clean after each application to prevent a watery build-up of medium that would otherwise splatter the artwork.*

3 *A second application of black completes the illusion of small apertures in the aluminium wheel. The tyre and body are both treated through separate fixed masks.*

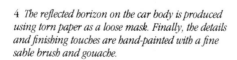

4 *The reflected horizon on the car body is produced using torn paper as a loose mask. Finally, the details and finishing touches are hand-painted with a fine sable brush and gouache.*

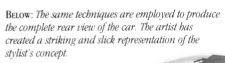

BELOW: *The same techniques are employed to produce the complete rear view of the car. The artist has created a striking and slick representation of the stylist's concept.*

BELOW: *A similar treatment for the front view of the vehicle shows how the airbrush can produce a far more realistic vision of an idea than other painting and drawing techniques allow.*

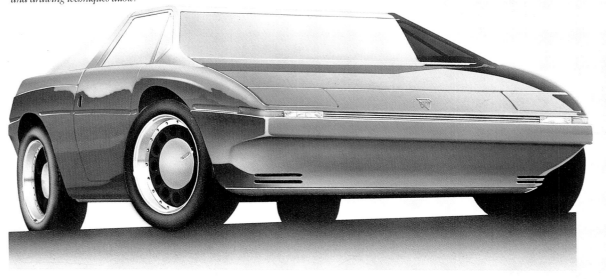

LOOSE MASKING

When a softer finish to an accurately defined edge is required a loose mask can be used, and this can be made of almost any material. Thin card, acetate, paper or preformed stencils, such as French curves or ellipse templates, can all be used. Tracing paper reinforced with masking film is particularly useful since the chosen outline can be carefully drawn onto the tracing paper while it is held in place on the painting. This is then covered with film to strengthen it and to make it waterproof (so it will not cockle). The shape is then cut out on a board before returning it to the painting for use.

The main difference between fixed and loose masking is that the latter technique allows the sprayed colour to creep under the mask (which may be held close to or away from the painted surface), with the edge becoming softer the farther away the mask is moved. Other materials that have interesting natural textures can also be used as masks to spray over or around, such as cotton wool, gauze or wire mesh, while torn blotting paper, for example, produces good cloud shapes.

It is certain that you will use both fixed and loose masking techniques in almost every painting you do. In fact, much of the fun in airbrushing comes from developing your own individual way of manipulating the spray with clever masking procedures.

M/A/I/N/T/E/N/A/N/C/E

Total, thorough and regular cleaning is essential to the continued smooth running of your airbrush. There are no apologies here for repeating this again, because it really is very important that you make a habit of taking care of what is, after all, an extremely delicate and vulnerable piece of equipment.

Get to know your airbrush inside and out, and understand its workings, so you can diagnose faults quickly when they occur. Luckily, although delicate and having fine tolerances, airbrushes are not complex pieces of machinery. They can be serviced and well-maintained with only a few basic tools – and a certain dexterity of fingerwork. If you avoid accidents and always keep the airbrush clean, the most you will ever be required to do is change the nozzle set or needle, which is simple enough. For major overhauls, your supplier or the manufacturer will put you in touch with a service agent.

CLEANING

A simple procedure for cleaning the airbrush as you work should be followed at each colour change, or if you are going to leave the airbrush standing for even a few minutes while working.

Blow out any remaining colour from the reservoir into a plastic bag, by closing the bag around the spray nozzle. This prevents the spray from polluting the air with paint droplets. (Always keep a plastic bag by the side of your work area, both for this job and also to hold messy paint-soaked tissues etc.) Fill the reservoir with water, or the required solvent if non-water-based colour was used, and blast this through until it runs clear. Ease a hair or bristle paint brush around the corners of the colour cup to remove stubborn sediment. The final blast of water or solvent can be sprayed into tissue or the palm of your hand (if it is not a harmful solvent) with the nozzle touching but the needle retracted, so that the nozzle cavity is cleared of any remaining traces of paint.

A final scrutiny of the airbrush at the end of a day's work is a

RIGHT: *There is an endless variety of material that can be used to form a mask. Indeed, anything solid or impervious to the medium is suitable. Traditionally, rubber adhesive was applied to precut sheets of tracing paper to make a fixed mask. This complex procedure has been replaced by adhesive-backed masking film, which is available in roll or sheet form, in matt or gloss finish. Liquid masking is used for fine details, hair lines and intricate shapes. Sheets of acetate are useful as they can be cut to form accurate loose masks. A sharp scalpel is essential for clean cuts in any masking material, and a steel ruler provides the best and safest cutting edge.*

ABOVE: *One of the most stylistic and powerful propaganda posters of World War II,* On to Japan *by the French artist Sevek. While the outlines to each component part of the graphic image have been created with fixed masks, simple loose masks and free-hand work added the tonal rendering within each element.*

good practice that ensures nothing is left to harden overnight and cause frayed nerves the next time you sit down to work.

At fairly regular intervals, the airbrush should be partly dismantled to give it a more thorough cleaning and to check how the needle and nozzle are wearing. Do this carefully and methodically by firstly unscrewing the handle and then the knurled needle screw. Withdraw the needle partly and unscrew and remove the nozzle assembly, so that the needle can now be pushed in at the rear and gently pulled out from the front.

Examine the needle tip and nozzle components using a magnifying glass. If very hooked, the needle must be replaced, but a slightly bent tip can be straightened by gently rolling it back and forth on a smooth, flat surface. This is also a good time to clear the needle of stains, which attract a build-up of paint if not dealt with from time to time. Hold a tissue soaked in cleaning solution under the needle while it is gently rotated to remove any stains left behind after flushing. The nozzle also needs to be pampered when dismantled. A quick soaking in cleaning solution, and then some attention with a fine sable brush will get rid of any built-up staining that may have occurred. An old needle can be gently inserted into the nozzle to loosen and clear any blockages, but no force should be applied or else the tip of the nozzle could be damaged. Examine the tip of the nozzle closely under a magnifying glass. If it is bent, closed over in

A B I E R T O by Ben Johnson

*Here, hard edges to the contrasting light and dark
elements of this painting have been created with fixed
film masking. Loose masks were used to represent the
softer textures of the curtain fabric. Fine details were
hand-painted.*

ABOVE: *This painting by Chris Moore of a somewhat unnatural human eye has a photographic quality. The total absence of hard edges increases the realism of the subject matter and the highly-finished image was produced with loose masks. The details were added using a tight free-hand control of the airbrush.*

Maintenance and cleaning *Careful and correct cleaning of the airbrush is essential to its continued smooth running and to prolong the life expectancy of its component parts. These illustrations show how one type of airbrush, with a 'floating' nozzle, is properly maintained. Use it as a guide — individual airbrushes call for a slightly different approach to dismantling, depending on their construction. Always refer to the manufacturers' drawings and instructions if in doubt.*

Hold the airbrush firmly and unscrew the handle 1. Loosen the needle-locking nut 2 and withdraw the needle into the body slightly. Remove the nozzle air cap 3, push the needle through the airbrush body and withdraw it carefully from the front 4. Take the air cap 5 and 6 and separate the guard from it 7. Clean all paint from both parts. Remove the floating nozzle from the airbrush body 8, making sure the rubber 'O' ring is removed with it. Separate the 'O' ring from the nozzle 9 and 10. Clean the nozzle by soaking in water or the appropriate solution 11. If traces of paint remain in the nozzle, use an old needle to carefully remove the old pigment 12. Replace the 'O' ring and insert the nozzle back into the body 13. Replace the air cap assembly 14 and inspect the colour cup for paint fragments 15. Rotate the wetted needle in the palm of the hand 16 to loosen any ingrained colour and then carefully slide the needle into position 17 – do not force. Tighten the locking nut 18. Reset the cam ring, if necessary, 19 and reset for normal use with the lever as far forward as possible 20.

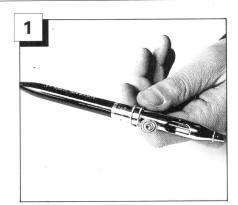

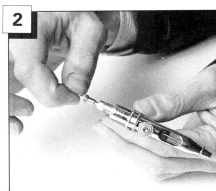

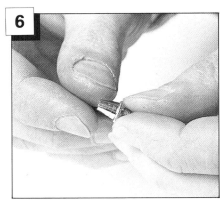

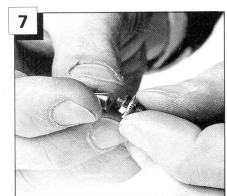

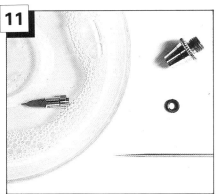

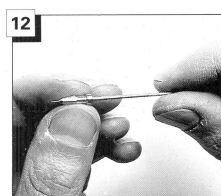

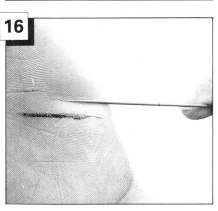

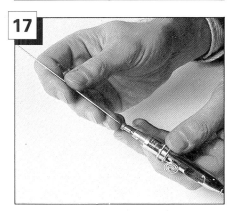

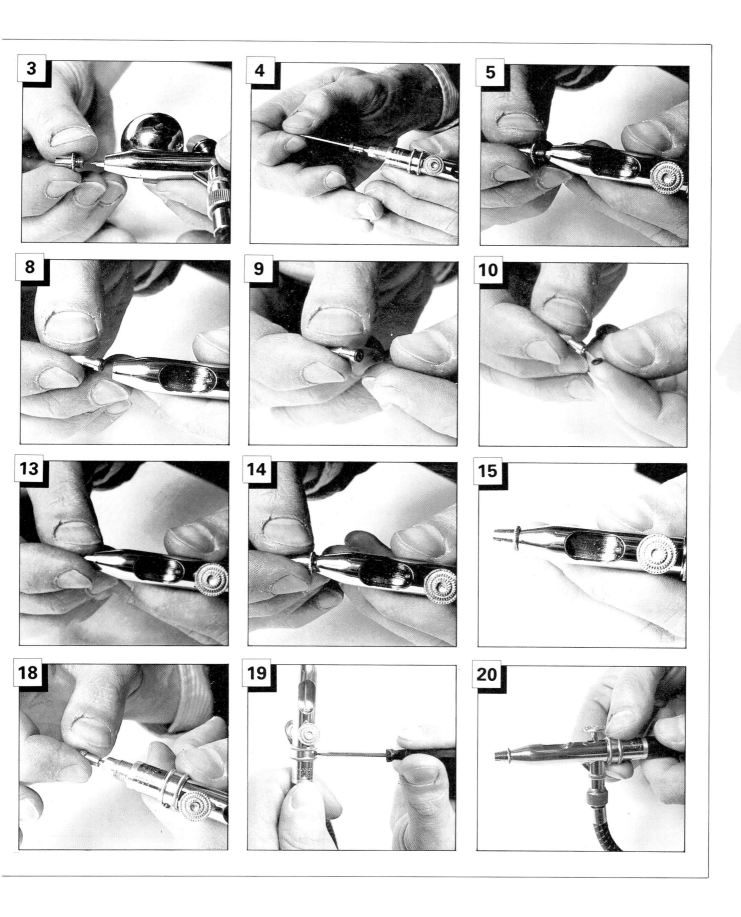

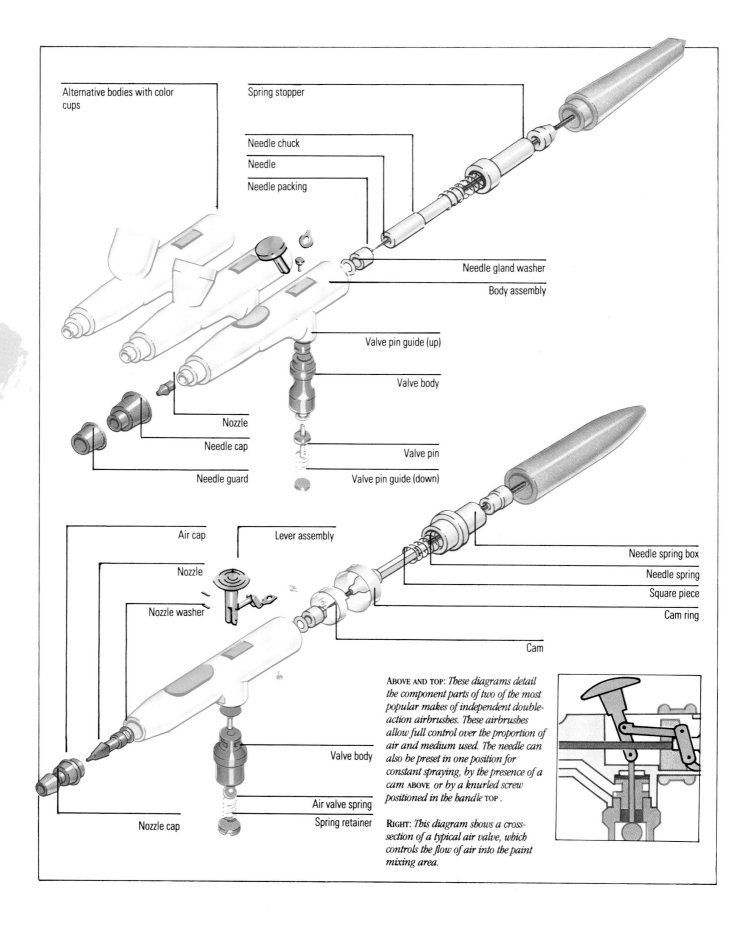

Alternative bodies with color cups

Spring stopper

Needle chuck

Needle

Needle packing

Needle gland washer

Body assembly

Valve pin guide (up)

Valve body

Nozzle

Needle cap

Valve pin

Needle guard

Valve pin guide (down)

Air cap

Lever assembly

Needle spring box

Needle spring

Square piece

Cam ring

Nozzle

Nozzle washer

Cam

Valve body

Air valve spring

Nozzle cap

Spring retainer

ABOVE AND TOP: *These diagrams detail the component parts of two of the most popular makes of independent double-action airbrushes. These airbrushes allow full control over the proportion of air and medium used. The needle can also be preset in one position for constant spraying, by the presence of a cam ABOVE or by a knurled screw positioned in the handle TOP .*

RIGHT: *This diagram shows a cross-section of a typical air valve, which controls the flow of air into the paint mixing area.*

F/A/U/L/T/-/F/I/N/D/I/N/G C/H/A/R/T

SPATTERING

Paint too thick or air pressure too low. — Adjust as required

Dirty or damaged nozzle or needle. — Examine both with a magnifying glass. Replace if damaged, clean thoroughly if dirty.

SPATTERING IN ONE DIRECTION

Bent needle or split nozzle. — Examine both and replace any damaged part.

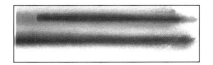

BLOBS AT BEGINNING OR END OF STROKES

Hand stationary at beginning or end of strokes. — Move your hand, release air, and then release paint when beginning a line. End a line in reverse order.

SPIDERS OR CENTIPEDES

Airbrush too close to ground for needle setting. — Allow less paint through when working close in.

Medium too diluted or air pressure too high. — Adjust either or both accordingly.

UNEVEN LINES

Pulsing from small direct compressor. — Make slower passes at the board. Fit moisture trap/air regulator.

Nozzle or needle dirty or damaged. — Check both, clean or replace parts.

FINE LINES TENDING TO DIFFUSE AT EDGES

Needle or nozzle damaged. — Check both, replace any faulty parts.

any way or split then you should replace it. If the airbrush is of a type that has a matched nozzle assembly, then all the component parts should be changed. Make sure, when you have dismantled the nozzle, to remove the 'o'-ring, as well, if this is fitted in your type of airbrush. Otherwise, you can 'shoot it into orbit' by blasting air through the body of the airbrush while cleaning it. Many wasted hours can be spent on hands and knees searching a studio for an 'o'-ring that is next to invisible.

To re-assemble the airbrush, work in reverse order, carefully slide the needle backward down the airbrush, finally pulling it from the rear until the tip is behind the nozzle aperture. Replace the nozzle assembly, then slide the needle forward until it sits comfortably in the nozzle, before tightening the needle-locking screw and replacing the handle.

If replacement parts are necessary, be sure to use only ones specifically intended for your make and model of airbrush. And remember that constant care and attention to your airbrush will mean a happier, more prolonged, and ultimately less expensive working relationship between the two of you.

BASIC TECHNIQUES

2

L/E/A/R/N/I/N/G T/O H/A/N/D/L/E T/H/E A/I/R/B/R/U/S/H

To use an airbrush well, and to the full extent of its capabilities, it is necessary to familiarize yourself with it and its individual characteristics. It is probably true to say that it takes more dexterity to produce a mark with an airbrush than with any traditional painting or drawing implement. The most obvious distinction between the airbrush and these other tools is the lack of physical contact between it and the surface on which the mark is made. Since this will be a new experience you must learn to control these marks, created by fractional movements of your hand, *before* they are propelled onto a surface. The best way to learn is by repeated exercise.

EXERCISE 1: DRY RUN

Smoothness is the key word with airbrushing — it is synonymous with the very nature of airbrush art and is achieved with time and practise. Once the airbrush and hand become one, and the spray pattern required has only to be visualized for the desired effect to be produced, success is assured. Many newcomers panic slightly the first time they have paint in their airbrush. The hiss of escaping air seems to precipitate action, which invariably leads to the release of large amounts of paint, producing blobs of colour where least expected. Beware, if the trigger is pulled back before being pressed down for air, the result will be an uncontrolled gush of paint. It is as well, therefore, to start with a few dry runs without any medium in the airbrush, just to acquaint yourself with your new equipment.

MATERIALS:
AN AIRBRUSH, WITH CONNECTING HOSE
AIR SUPPLY

1 Hold the airbrush like a pen, between thumb and middle finger, with your index finger on the trigger. Move the trigger back and forth, and up and down, getting used to its feel and spring pressure.

2 Think the process of spraying through: press down on the trigger for air – pull back on the trigger for paint.

3 Do this while moving your hand to and fro at a steady distance a few inches above your work surface, again with air being fed through to get used to the sound of the airbrush at work. Generally try to eliminate any stiffness in your movement.

1 *Press down for air.*   2 *Pull back gently for paint.*   3 *Ease trigger forward at end of each stroke.*   4 *Finally release trigger.*

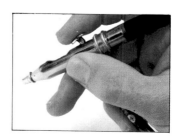

EXERCISE 2: DOODLES

When using paint in the airbrush for the first time concentrate on simple tests and exercises and become acquainted with the action of spraying. Spend a little time doodling on sheets of scrap paper to build up your confidence.

MATERIALS:
PAINT MEDIUM
SEVERAL, LARGE, SHEETS OF WHITE DRAWING PAPER
CLEAN WATER
TISSUES

1 Set up your airbrush, connecting it securely to the air hose, and with the air pressure set at 30 psi (2 bar).

2 Take your chosen medium, mixing it, if necessary, to the correct consistency, and transfer a small amount to the airbrush colour cup. Either use a dropper or the brush you used to mix the paint, provided it is clean and does not have a tendency to shed hairs. Do not overfill the cup, and make sure that when you hold the airbrush toward the paper, fluid does not pour out. If any colour does get onto the outside of the airbrush, remove it with a tissue before it is able to run down to the nozzle area, otherwise it could be blown onto your artwork.

3 Start with the airbrush 2 in (5 cm) away from the paper, press down the trigger while at the same time beginning to move your arm sideways and then pull the trigger back to release paint. By beginning to move the airbrush before allowing paint through, you will avoid blobs appearing at the start of the line.

4 At the end of each stroke, ease the trigger forward to shut off the paint supply before you have stopped moving the airbrush. This is a very elementary and essential lesson. You will probably not get it right straight away, but mastering it will be at the heart of most of your airbrush work.

5 During those doodle sessions, experiment with the distance between airbrush and paper, and the amounts of paint allowed through. You will find that close in to the sheet a dense, well-defined line can be made, while farther away the same paint supply will make a broader, lighter band of colour with very soft edges. Also, you will begin to gauge how much colour can be allowed through when working in close, before the paper becomes too wet and the paint is blown away in runs forming a distinctive 'centipede'.

Once you have spent a little time making simple marks on paper and have become more familiar and less hesitant with your airbrush, it is time to apply yourself to some basic exercises that will give you more specific control over the airbrush.

EXERCISE 3: LINE CONTROL

This exercise will help you to progress from the freehand lines you made in your doodles to lines of specific dimensions, from very dense lines to broad diffused ones, and in doing so will increase your ability to control the airbrush.

MATERIALS:
AS FOR EXERCISE 2, PLUS:
PENCIL
RULER

1 On your paper, draw two vertical pencil lines about 10 in (25 cm) apart. These are boundaries between which your airbrushed lines should be constant. Place a ruler horizontally across these lines and lift the far edge slightly to use as a guide along which the airbrush can run while spraying a line onto the paper.

2 Starting 2 in (5 cm) to the left of the left-hand boundary, begin moving to the right, with the airflow on, then allow the paint through. By the time you cross the boundary the paint/air mixture should be established, and then maintained until the second boundary is crossed, when you should allow the trigger forward, then upward before ending the stroke.

3 Move down the sheet, producing gradually broader lines by manipulating the paint supply and distance to the paper. The ruler will eventually limit the width of your spray, but you can continue with broader strokes working freehand.

EXERCISE 4: DOT CONTROL

The object of this exercise is to give you practice in spraying a small, precise dot of colour. This discipline is useful to acquaint you with fine degrees of trigger control, and will also develop the skill which will enable you to add freehand touches to the smallest of details. That skill is to aim accurately and to tease exactly the right amount of paint out of the airbrush.

MATERIALS:
LARGE SHEET OF BLACK PAPER
WHITE GOUACHE
OLD TOOTHBRUSH

1 Take an old, clean toothbrush and dip the ends of its bristles into some white gouache. (This can be thicker than you would use in your airbrush, but be sure to thin it adequately for the rest of the exercise.) By gently pulling back the bristles with the fingertip, lightly spatter the paper to produce a 'star-scape'. Allow to dry.

2 Now, with white paint in the airbrush and working from close up to 2 in (5 cm) away from the surface, add a white 'glow' to the 'stars'. The larger the star, the bigger the glow, so work farther away from the paper to achieve this variation in size.

You will find this task easier if you aim, keeping the air on, while gently easing the trigger backward and forward very slightly, gradually allowing the colour to build up. Too much colour at once will over-wet the surface and be blown into a spidery leg, but careful air/paint control keeps the surface dry after each tiny addition of colour.

NOTE: The constant airflow and small paint consumption in this exercise dries out the nozzle quickly, so occasionally move to a piece of scrap paper and blast through a larger amount of colour to keep the opening of the nozzle from drying completely.

EXERCISE 5: FLAT TONE

This exercise is important as it will help you to acquire early on the ability to render a solid colour, perfectly flat and without blemishes. The capacity to perform this is one of the great advantages that the airbrush has over other painting techniques. From here on the exercises described will be best carried out on a surface more substantial than paper, since the masking techniques used will pluck and tear fibrous papers. Art board is the best material.

MATERIALS:
ART BOARD, 8 × 8 in (20 × 20 cm), OR LARGER
LIGHTER FLUID (CLEANING SOLVENT)
2H PENCIL
RULER
MASKING FILM
SCALPEL

1 De-grease the art board by wiping it with a tissue soaked in lighter fluid (cleaning solvent). (Keep all naked flames well out of the way when doing this.)

2 Draw a 6-in (15-cm) square on the board, making sure you keep your hands out of contact with the area to be sprayed.

3 Cut a piece of masking film to cover the square and its immediate surround, peel it from its backing sheet and pull it into place on the board before smoothing it down to eliminate any air bubbles.

4 With a sharp scalpel and a ruler, carefully cut out the square; be aware of the pressure you apply to the scalpel to avoid cutting the board's surface. Lift the cut masking film at one corner using the scalpel tip, and peel off that area.

5 You are now ready to spray. Load the colour cup and, holding the airbrush about 5–6 in (12–15 cm) from the board, begin spraying from left to right in fairly broad strokes, but without over-wetting. You will find that the board is less absorbent than paper and can be overloaded with paint much more easily. But with careful work you can spray horizontal lines across and back, with each one overlapping slightly to keep the tone uniform. Remember to take each stroke beyond the masking line before returning, otherwise an overly dense area of colour will result.

6 If you get a striped effect, turn the board through 90° and spray a similar pattern across the first layer. You may need to apply several layers of colour to achieve a totally flat tone.

7 Once the flat colour has been achieved, allow all the paint to dry naturally, both on the board and on the masking film. Do not try to rush this process by using a heater or hair dryer, as this can damage the masking film and adversely affect your work. When the paint has dried completely, remove the masking film to reveal a perfect square.

1 *Cut the masking film with a sharp scalpel.*

2 *Use the scalpel tip to raise a corner of the cut film.*

3 *Peel back the film.*

4 *Begin to build up a layer of flat tone, using several light passes rather than one heavy spray.*

5 *Allow the medium to dry between each application.*

6 *When dry, remove the masking film.*

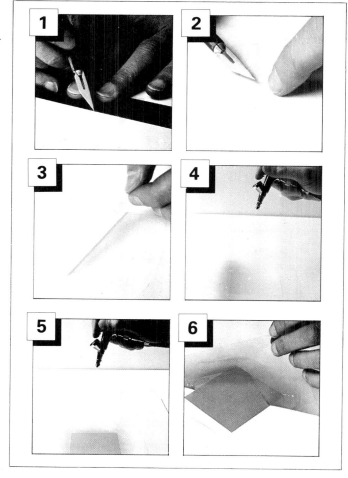

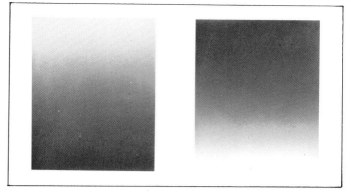

EXERCISE 6: GRADED TONE

The perfect graduation of one tone into another is the quintessence of airbrushing. To achieve a perfect vignette over a large area is one of the tasks most frequently demanded of airbrush artists, and therefore one that must be practiced and mastered at this early stage. It may take several attempts to achieve a satisfactory finish, but perseverence will be rewarded by an increase in the standard of all subsequent airbrush work.

It is generally accepted that inks are the easiest medium to use for this job since their transparency means that a tint of the colour can be created by light, even spraying, while several layers will build up into a solid colour. With gouache, however, a tonal palette is needed where several tints of the main colour are mixed. These are sprayed from dark to light, each in turn blending smoothly with the previous tint – in effect, a number of smaller vignettes are used to produce an overall gradation. The aim of this exercise is to produce a vignette that descends from a solid colour at the top, to a 10% tint of the colour at the bottom.

MATERIALS:
AS FOR EXERCISE 5, PLUS
INKS, AND REQUIRED SOLVENTS

1 Prepare some art board as before, but change the square to a rectangle 7 × 5 in (18 × 12 cm). Mask this area off, and, with a strong colour of ink in the airbrush, begin spraying from the top.

2 To achieve the solid colour you must begin quite close to the board (about 2 in (5 cm) distance would be about right). Working from side to side, slightly overlapping each stroke with the previous one as you work down the board into the lighter tones.

3 As you descend, still moving side to side, you must do two things to lighten the tone – lessen the supply of medium at each pass, while also moving the airbrush away from the board. Obviously, because of the nature of the effect, you cannot turn the board through 90° as in the previous exercise, and so much greater care is needed to graduate the colour. You can work on it the other way around, though, with the darkest tone nearest you, working away to the lighter areas. However, you will find that the airstream will blow an overspray ahead of the airbrush depositing some colour where the lighter tints will be. This affects their density, and is particularly unacceptable if fading the colour out to pure white.

4 Try repeating this exercise using gouache and a tonal palette as described. Mix the paint for the solid colour, and also for a middle and light tint of it. Carefully spray the darkest colour first, grading it down the board to about half way before feathering it out. Clean out the airbrush and refill with the middle tint, blending it into the first and again feathering it out before the bottom of the board. Finally, using the lightest tint in the cleaned airbrush, complete the vignette.

S/P/R/A/Y/I/N/G S/I/M/P/L/E F/O/R/M/S

The previous six exercises have been designed to help build up your ability to control the airbrush throughout its range of capabilities, and while you will never stop learning different ways of manipulating its effects, you should by now be competent enough to begin representational work. The following few exercises in basic forms and textures will test your control by putting the abstract lessons you have learned into closely defined parameters. Whereas before you merely had to make the correct mark, now you must put the correct mark in the correct place – a simple enough distinction to write down, but rather more difficult to achieve. The key, as always with this work, is not to rush anything. You should move at your own pace, completing each of the four solid forms at least once, but repeating the exercise for any that you have difficulty with.

The basic forms demonstrated here embody all the shapes that make up our world. That is to say, any object or form that we know is a compound of the curves and planes found in the sphere, the cone, the cylinder and the cube. The exercises that follow will first show you how to describe these curves and planes by depicting light and shadow. Visually describing these in two dimensions is the key to achieving the illusion of solidity and depth. Once the representation of solidity has been mastered, you will have to consider the surface qualities of texture, reflectivity and colour.

MATERIALS:
ART BOARD, 8 × 8 in (20 × 20 cm), OR LARGER
LIGHTER FLUID (CLEANING SOLVENT)
2H PENCIL
RULER
MASKING FILM
SCALPEL
INKS
STIFF PAPER FOR LOOSE MASKING
ELLIPSE TEMPLATE

EXERCISE 7: THE CUBE

Of the four shapes to be tackled, the cube is the simplest form to render as a solid object using light and shadow, since its flat faces and straight edges can be drawn, masked and sprayed with relative ease. It is therefore sensible to begin with the cube as described below.

1 Draw the outline of a cube onto a de-greased art board, as shown here. A reasonable size for the purpose of this exercise would be about 6 in (15 cm) across.

2 Lay some masking film across the drawing and cut along all of the nine lines that comprise the cube, and then lift away the lower right-hand section of film, placing it onto its backing sheet temporarily. Because of the simplicity of the shape it will be possible to re-use each piece of masking film to cover and protect the area that it was removed from.

3 Using black for your colour, load the airbrush and prepare to apply tone to the exposed area. Since the darkest tone will be most prominent visually, and therefore seem closest to the viewer, the fore and top edges of the side should be rendered darkest, receding back to a mid-tone at the lower rear corner.

4 Use the experience you gained in Exercise 6 to achieve this diagonal vignette. When you feel that the section is completed, allow it to dry thoroughly, then carefully re-position the removed piece of mask.

5 Now remove the lower left-hand piece of mask and apply tone across this face. Remember that you have already completed the darkest face, the one most in shadow, so use colour more sparingly on this side, vignetting down from the top edge.

6 Replace the second piece of mask, uncover the top plane of the cube and spray a very light tone on the point furthest away from you to pick out the back edges from the white background of the board; the cube is now complete.

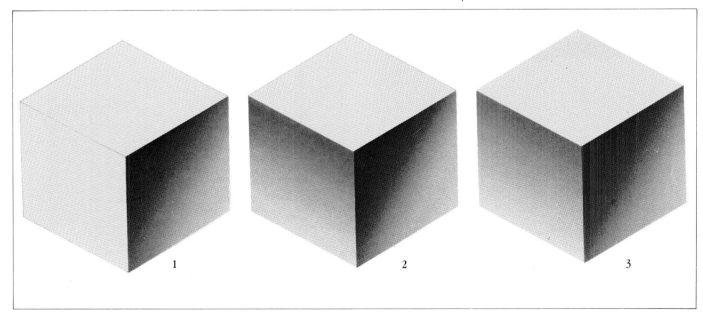

1   2   3

RIGHT: Sphere 1 *The sphere is created with a single fixed mask. Once uncovered, the area is treated with an arcing application of medium. 2 As the shadow builds up the sphere appears more solid. 3 A loose mask completes the effect by suggesting a slight reflection below.*

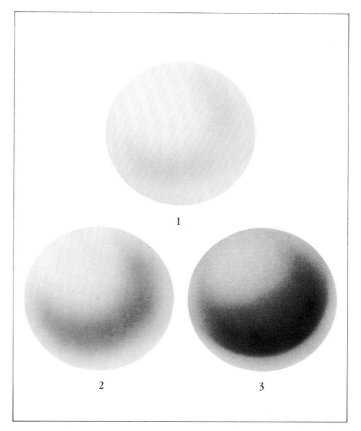

EXERCISE 8: THE SPHERE

Achieving the impression of a solid-looking sphere is rewarding to the beginner because it demonstrates a greater control over the airbrush than any of the previous exercises require. It is the first time that a curved vignette has been demanded, the first time that complete strokes are laid down *within* the boundaries of a mask, and also the first time that a loose mask has been required.

LEFT: Cube 1 *The right-hand panel of the cube is revealed and sprayed diagonally. The masking film is then replaced. 2 Masking film is removed from the left-hand panel and the second vignette is applied from top to bottom. 3 The top panel is finally given a light vignette from top to bottom.*

1 Draw a 4-in (10-cm) diameter circle on your board, and cover with some masking film. Using an adapted compass with a scalpel blade securely gripped in the inking attachment, lightly retrace the circle, cutting the film as you go. Remove the circle of film.

2 Imagine a light source coming from behind your left shoulder, and begin to lay down a very fine tone around the circle leaving a highlight in its upper left quadrant. It is important to keep your spray away from this area from now on, to retain the highlight, while working a curved vignette to describe the spherical form.

3 Carefully spray below and to the right of the highlight, tapering off the spray as you reach either end of the inverted arc that your hand and airbrush should be describing.

4 Once this area builds up to a mid-tone, it is necessary to use a loose mask to protect the very underside of the sphere and to prevent it from going black. For this mask cut another circle from stiff paper, this time with a 3½ in (9 cm) diameter, leaving a circle template to hold inside of the original film mask. Continue to build up the darkest tone, manipulating the loose mask to ensure that a soft edge is created, and so create the illusion that the sphere recedes underneath.

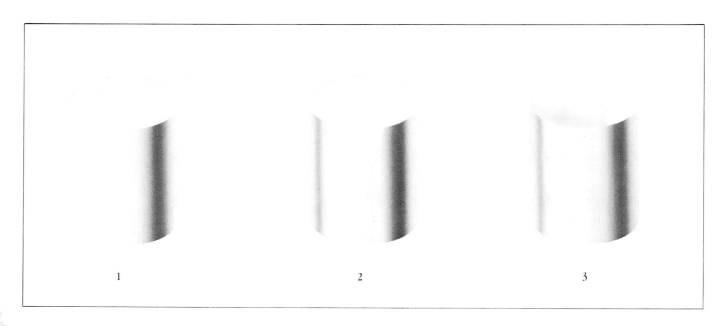

1   2   3

ABOVE: Cylinder *This form requires two areas of fixed masking.* 1 *The front, curving face is revealed first and vertical bands of shadow and tone applied to suggest volume.* 2 *A ruler is again used as a loose mask and as a guide for the airbrush to add a further band of shadow. The front face is remasked.* 3 *The top face is revealed and sprayed as a simple vignette.*

EXERCISE 9: THE CYLINDER

The characteristic banding of tone used to create the illusion of a curving tubular surface can be illustrated quite simply by picking out a highlight band and countering that with bands of heavy shading. The more reflective you wish to make the surface, the harder-edged and more complicated does this banding become, but for a simple tonal study the following method will prove successful.

1 On a board, draw a vertical line with two horizontals crossing it, some 3 in (7 cm) apart, using the finest pencil lines you can make. With these as the axes, draw a complete isometric ellipse over the upper intersection of lines, and the bottom half of a similar ellipse over the base. Join up the extreme ends of the major axes with the two vertical lines to create a cylinder.

2 Cover the drawing with masking film and cut out the shapes. As with the cube, there should be no difficulty in replacing these simple masks and so the job can be done with one piece of film. Remove the mask from the curved wall of the cylinder, and store it on its original backing sheet.

3 Imagine where your highlight should fall, making it a band of white just to the left of the centre line. It will now be easier to work with the cylinder horizontal in front you, so turn the board 90° so that the banding goes from left to right.

4 Using a ruler as a loose mask and holding it a little way from the board, spray a light band of colour either side of your imagined highlight band, keeping the edges soft but parallel.

5 Next, using the ruler as a guide on which to rest the chin of the airbrush nozzle, make a broad dark band along the shadowed side of the cylinder, leaving a mid-tone at the extreme edge where the curved side recedes away. A final dark narrow band to the left (when upright) of the cylinder completes the impression of the curving surface.

6 Replace the first mask and remove the elliptical end mask to spray a tone to describe this surface, putting down a little more paint in the area adjacent to the highlight band.

ABOVE: Cone 1 *The cone shape is masked and a light tone sprayed leaving a highlight section. 2 A dark shadow is created using a ruler as a loose mask. 3 Finally, a second, reflective shadow is added to complete the form.*

EXERCISE 10: THE CONE

In many ways the treatment for producing a cone is similar to that for the cylinder, except that a little more loose masking is required, and care is needed to make the bands of tone converge to a point. These steps will help you create the required image.

1 Draw a vertical line with a low horizontal to cross it, and with an ellipse template draw the base of the cone. Take two lines from a point on the vertical to meet the ellipse at right and left and your cone is drawn.

2 Apply some masking film over the board, cut out and reveal the cone shape.

3 Use a ruler as a loose mask, being careful to ensure that the airbrushed tone will converge exactly with the tip of the cone, and spray a light tone on either side of an imagined highlight band.

4 Again using the ruler as a mask, darken the shadow side of the cone, tapering the spray pattern by pulling your airbrush hand back over the ruler as you move toward the tip. Make a similar but narrower band on the other side of the highlight to complete the effect.

EXERCISE 11: TEXTURE AND COLOUR

This is really a series of exercises, relying upon your imaginative, interpretive and visual skills as much as upon your airbrushing abilities to make them succeed.

The end result of the previous four exercises was a tonal rendering of all the basic geometric forms. They gave a strong impression of solidity, and because of the virtues of the airbrushing technique, did so in a way that made them very believable. However, they did not describe anything other than a form. This is a very necessary and worthwhile achievement, but one which falls short of reality. To move on from this impression of solidity to suggest reality, another aspect needs to be described. This is the nature of the material from which forms are made.

This description of form involves colour, texture, density, the reflectiveness of its external surface and the effect of a light source or sources playing upon it. All of these factors help give an object its visual identity, and the ability to interpret and translate this information into two dimensions in a way that others can understand is fundamental.

There are many materials from which the cube, cylinder, sphere and cone could be made, and probably just as many ways for each type of material to be illustrated. There are also many techniques, mostly stylizations – simplifications designed to be easily understood rather than be literally truthful – by which they can be represented. It is necessary to have to decide whether or not to accept the pre-determined stylizations, some of which may have become tired clichés, or whether to experiment and discover individual methods of describing these materials. The examples in this exercise are themselves simple and very basic stylizations based on a few everyday materials. They are your first chance to experiment with colour in your airbrush, which is the reason for their being so uncomplicated. As time goes by and your ability improves, you may find their simplicity unacceptable in your own work. It is to be hoped that this will be the case, but for now try any of the examples shown, adding perhaps a few materials of your own.

MATERIALS:
ALL PREVIOUS MATERIALS
A FULL RANGE OF COLOURS

MATT STEEL

A simple start this, since the material being described has no striking characteristics, other than its dull metallic sheen, and so it can be dealt with using soft vignettes with no masking other than for the outline shapes. You should spray the dark grey tones first, leaving a fair amount of contrast, which can then be filled and softened by a more bluey tone.

CHROME

Chrome, being bright and reflective but without a general colour of its own is chameleon-like in nature, taking on the colours of its surroundings, and reflecting back a distorted version of the objects around it. This can be a commotion of visual imagery in reality, so a simplication is often required with only the sky, in a rich blue, a dark, often black horizon, and a smooth vignette of browns to represent the ground around it. This still requires foresight, or research, to describe where these elements begin and end on any one shape, otherwise the effect will be less than convincing. The high degree of reflectiveness in the surface demands sharp contrasts between light and dark areas, so fixed masking or else a loose mask held tightly against the artwork will be needed to create the division between sky and horizon.

GLASS

The examples of glass shown are over-simplified to help you experiment and understand the problems of ghosting-in the reverse sides of the forms. Placing a glass object in an environment would require a great deal of thought into how other objects may look through it or indeed how they would affect its appearance. Experiment first of all by presuming the glass is in a white void; this way you can concentrate on the blue and green hues within, and the receding edges. Care has to be taken to ensure that the distant edges do recede visually otherwise an uncomfortable 'reversing' illusion will occur. Stark highlights, such as the reflection of window frames can be added by fixed masking, and will help enhance the illusion of the surface being shiny.

RUBBER

Rubber, like other manufactured materials, can be produced in any form, with many different textures, depending upon the compound used. The example shown here suggests a very soft, spongy texture, hence the lack of a high sheen on the surface. The texture has been achieved with a spatter cap, but if your airbrush does not have this facility, experimenting with very low air pressures, or even using the toothbrush method of spattering, can produce a similar effect. The black used as a base colour has been complemented with the addition of scarlet to give warmth and body to the texture.

STONE

It can be great fun experimenting with spatter techniques within a masked-off shape, and always a joy when the masking is removed to see the effect against a background of other textures. The portrayal of stone objects gives you the opportunity to exploit the technique fully, and studying just a few examples of stone, brick, or rock will show you that almost every colour can be found in the material. The

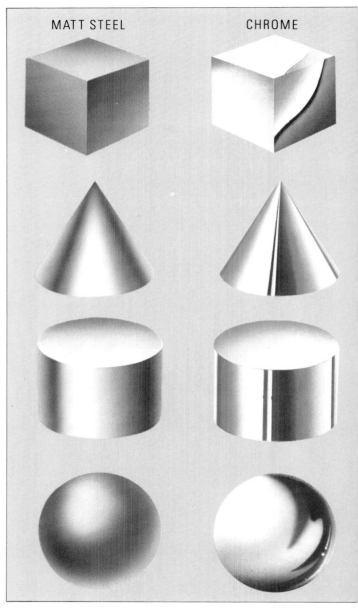

MATT STEEL   CHROME

examples shown here are built up with yellow ochre and grey spatter, with tonal shading added using the airbrush normally. White paint spattered as a finishing touch will give the diffused highlight that is common in worked stone.

WOOD

By studying wooden objects around you, the myriad ranges of colour, texture and graining to be found will give you an idea of the complexity of the material. Simplification of these qualities, and experimentation with various loose masking techniques, freehand work, hand painting and even coloured pencil detailing will help to create the effect of rough or finished wood. Spraying a light base colour with attention to tonal shading provides the foundation on which the detail can be built. Cutting a wavy line down a piece of paper and pulling it apart to form a small gap will make a useful loose mask for this purpose.

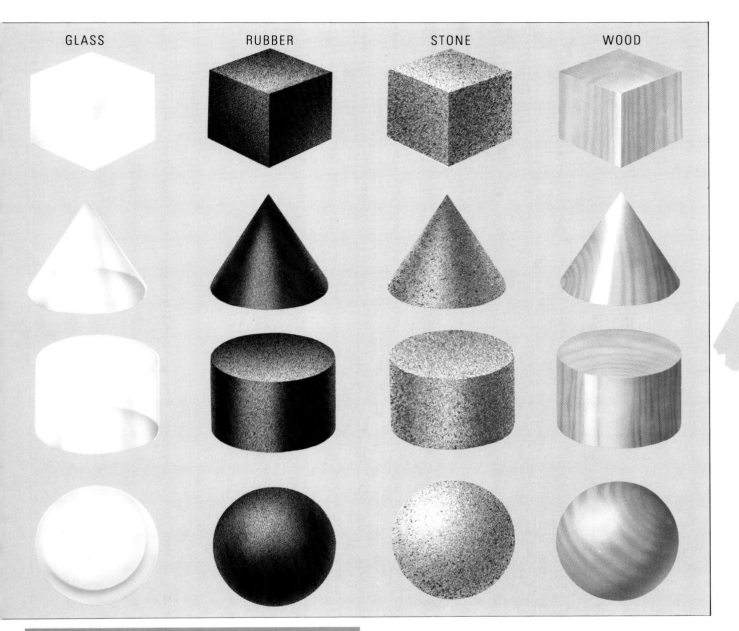

GLASS   RUBBER   STONE   WOOD

B/U/I/L/D/I/N/G U/P A D/R/A/W/I/N/G

The previous exercises have demanded very little from you in the way of drawing, so it was possible to work directly onto the surface of the art board when producing your outline shapes prior to airbrushing in the colour. From now on, however, as the work you produce becomes more involved as far as shape and number of elements are concerned, it will be necessary to work up a drawing to finished standards before transferring it onto the art board. This is to protect the board from being overworked, and from being damaged by drawing instruments, pencils and erasures.

Also, if you tried to build up a drawing directly on the board, no matter how scrupulous you were with hand-washing, it would be impossible to avoid leaving traces of skin oils each time hands and fingers made contact with it, and these traces would resist and repel the airbrush colours. It is far better to make your mistakes, correct them, build up the drawn image, perhaps experiment with the composition of its component parts and then finally trace off the resulting design and transfer it to the art board.

The method of building up the drawing will depend largely upon the sort of work you produce now and would like to produce with the airbrush. A tried and trusted formula with many artists is to work on progressively more finished drawings using sheets of layout paper, which because of its light weight is fairly transparent. By this means a quick rendering of a subject that has pleasing elements in it may be redrawn with greater accuracy and with non-essential marks eliminated onto a sheet of paper placed over the first. Outside elements, drawn separately, can also be brought in and moved around before their size and position is finally fixed and then incorporated in a later drawing. The end result of this procedure is an accurate outline drawing of the component parts of your proposed painting that is ready to be traced onto the waiting art board.

A great number of airbrush artists and illustrators who have been drawn to the technique by its abilities to make photographic likenesses, need photographic reference material to produce their work, often pooling this material from several sources in a composite picture. For them to sit and repeatedly sketch from their reference material until a photographic accuracy has been achieved would be foolish and time consuming. Their art lies in the esoteric manipulation of available images to produce an unavailable new reality or hyper-reality within their work, and in this they are justified in tracing directly from photographic reference.

This does not mean that an airbrush artist does not need good drawing skills, nor does it mean that the technique will hide bad drawing. The reason that airbrushing has, in the past, been seen in a bad light in certain quarters is that many less talented people have tried to hide their artistic weaknesses and inabilities behind the strong effects that the technique offers. Luckily with the wealth of talent now involved in the airbrush world, the reputation of its art has largely been saved, and at the same time the general standard of work has been boosted.

Meanwhile, your own work has to be of the highest standard that you can maintain at each stage and with each painting, and so the drawing stage is as important to the finished painting as is the airbrushing. Your ultimate aim must be to produce an accurate outline drawing, precisely detailing each component part of your picture that will be masked off and coloured when it is transferred to the board.

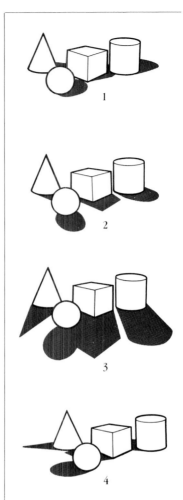

T/R/A/C/I/N/G D/O/W/N

When you have your final rough, it should be taped firmly and flatly to your drawing board with a sheet of tracing paper taped over it. Recommended for this task is smooth natural tracing paper of 90gsm weight. Thinner materials can tear too easily.

Using a 2H to 4H pencil, kept sharp at all times for clarity and accuracy, make a trace of the image you have produced.

There are two ways to transfer this tracing to your art board now. Firstly, you could use a transfer paper, which is an intermediary between board and tracing. Also known as rouge paper, this is a sheet of thin paper coated on one side with a fine red powder. A new sheet must be thoroughly wiped down with dry tissues to remove excess dust, and then it can be placed face down on the art board with the tracing on top, taped down flat. Using a sharp 8H pencil pencil the image can be traced off leaving a light red line on the board to work to. Alternatively, a less harassing method is to simply scribble all over the back of your tracing with the flat of a 2H pencil, and then in small circular motions rub this in with a wad of cotton wool until any loose graphite has gone and the surface has become uniform and shiny. Tracing down, as before with an 8H pencil, will leave a light grey line, which is often more acceptable, if it should peep through the finished airbrushing, than a red line can be.

EXERCISE 12: GEOMETRIC STILL LIFE

When you have tried several of the examples in the previous exercise and feel confident to proceed, a final useful step before launching

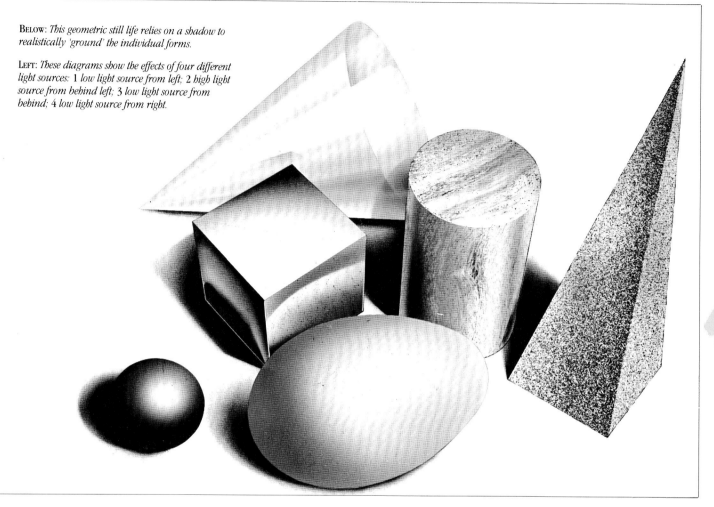

BELOW: *This geometric still life relies on a shadow to realistically 'ground' the individual forms.*

LEFT: *These diagrams show the effects of four different light sources: 1 low light source from left; 2 high light source from behind left; 3 low light source from behind; 4 low light source from right.*

yourself on a full-blown project is a simple still life of the shapes and textures you have been working with. Tackled successfully, this exercise will help you on your way with more complicated jobs to come.

By working up your drawing beforehand with the methods previously described, you can produce an outline representation of the basic shapes in a realistic perspective. Add to this, with careful thought and experiment, shadows cast by the objects so that they 'sit' convincingly on the page.

Always remember to bear in mind the light direction and strength when creating your shadows. This will help to keep all the shadows consistent with each other and the light source, and when it comes to airbrushing in the colour you will also have a good idea of where to place the corresponding highlights on the solids. Apart from shadow, this exercise will give you the opportunity to illustrate the effect that objects have on each other. Even dull, matt surfaces will pick up a hint of colour from an object placed next to them. The airbrush is an ideal tool to create this effect, since a light tint of colour can be gently blown onto all or part of an object to give the impression that it is receiving or reflecting colour from nearby.

When you have made up your drawing and carefully traced it off onto 90gsm smooth tracing paper, as previously described, transfer it to a piece of de-greased art board. Starting with the rearmost object

and working forward, mask off and airbrush each one in turn. The shadows should all be dealt with in one go and can be added as a final stage. However, once they are complete, it may be necessary to add a little more tone to the objects, at least in some areas, in order to 'marry' the shading to the strength and direction of lighting suggested by your shadows.

Do not worry if you need to go back into the illustration to strengthen any mark you have made – learning is the whole point of these exercises and experience is the thing that will in future help you to get the effect right first time.

In the example of the exercise shown here, the basic shapes have been complemented with the addition of a stone pyramid and an egg. The perspective has been carefully created and checked to be visually correct. A quick and easy way to check a drawing for such a basic fault as incorrect perspective is to hold it up in front of a mirror. Because you have been staring at an overlooked fault for a long time it may have become accepted, but seeing it presented back to front will emphasize the defect and you will spot it immediately.

The shadows shown here have been created by loose masking while the solids were masked off with fixed film. The softness at the distant ends of the shadows, and their divergence from each other, suggests a fairly soft lighting in close proximity above and to the right of the group.

PROJECTS

3

This chapter opens up a vast range of new possibilities for you and your airbrush, as well as providing the opportunity to develop and extend your skills and abilities within the field. Seven projects are presented, each designed to build up gradually the expertise needed to devise and tackle new jobs of your own. The projects will also break down and remove the mystery behind the techniques most commonly found in airbrush art.

You are not required to imitate each project exactly. To do so might hinder your progress, for by setting a tried and true course the projects will prevent you making mistakes, and hence lose their educational value! Learning by trial and error is by far the best way to find your own style, and with it the confidence to explore new territory beyond that set out in this book. Instead, use these projects for their instructional value. They will provide a constant source of reference for solving problems long after your need for the general instruction they provide has ended.

F/O/R/W/A/R/D P/L/A/N/N/I/N/G

Before beginning any project, give some thought to the order in which to proceed, thereby minimizing mistakes or marks in areas that are difficult or impossible to work around. A lot of time can be wasted by launching into a project unprepared.

There are a few general and basic rules about the order in which the various stages of a painting can be completed, but they are not rigid and should be set aside rather than have them compromise an illustration. Like any rules in art they ultimately limit creativity, and therefore are at times best ignored.

It is up to you to develop your own ground rules; these will establish themselves along with your technique as you do more airbrush work. But until such a time as you can 'read' paintings before you begin them – seeing instinctively the best and most economical ways to proceed – you should consider working to these guidelines.

1 Where applicable, work on the background first. Whether sky, dark vignette or whatever, the background is a springboard from which the subject must jump. Painting it first leaves you in control of the presentation of the subject.

2 If using inks or watercolour, work from light to dark, since the darker tones cannot be lightened later when using a transparent medium.

3 Decide on the most economical method of masking, especially when using fixed masks and where possible avoid constantly remasking the same areas. Saving used masks until the work is completed is a good habit to develop, so that if an area requires further attention, the means are readily available.

4 Pay attention to the protection of painted areas that have already been completed.

5 When tracing a drawing down, do not make any marks that may show through the finished painting, for example where the colouring is light. Remember that when using matt masking film, parts of the drawing can be made on the film surface, thus providing a removable guide when adding detail.

P/R/O/J/E/C/T 1/:
S/T/I/L/L L/I/F/E

This project is a simple step forward from the exercises of the previous chapter. By applying the same skills that were used to create geometric forms, and by observing familiar objects like an apple and some bananas, you should be able to complete your first realistic project without much trouble.

One technique which is demonstrated here for the first time, and which will prove useful to you in the future, is that of preparing the basic form of the painting by adding a light monochrome airbrushed 'wash'. In doing this you not only give immediate substance to the picture on which to build the colour and details, but also it gives you the opportunity to prepare all the masks that will be used in the later stages. The project can be undertaken as follows:

1

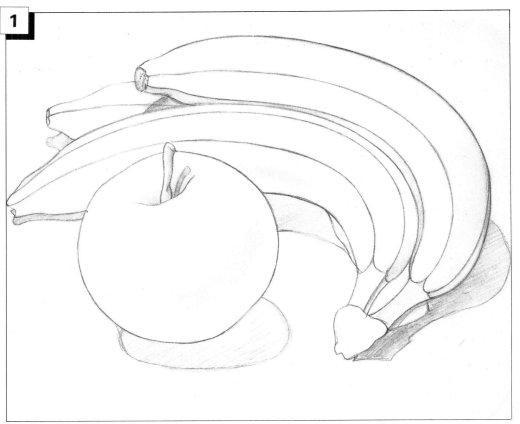

1 First of all prepare a drawing from a suitable reference, either photographic or, as is preferable in this case, from real life. Work on the drawing until all the forms are correctly realized, and then accurately copy them onto tracing paper using a sharp 2H pencil. Transfer the tracing to art board and cover the whole area with masking film.

2

2 Cut around the component parts of the image, then remove the mask from the apple, keeping the piece of masking film for later reuse. Mix a little black ink with water, add some to your airbrush reservoir, and spray in a light modelling tone to the shaded side of the apple. Using a piece of acetate, or alternatively tracing paper reinforced with masking film, cut a mask to add the dimple, stalk and dark spots to the apple. Replace the original mask over the apple, and remove the mask from the bananas, again retaining it for future use. Treat the bananas with the same light modelling process, making loose masks for shadows and details as and when required. When you have rendered both fruits successfully with light monochrome modelling washes, you will be able to proceed with building up colour and detail.

3

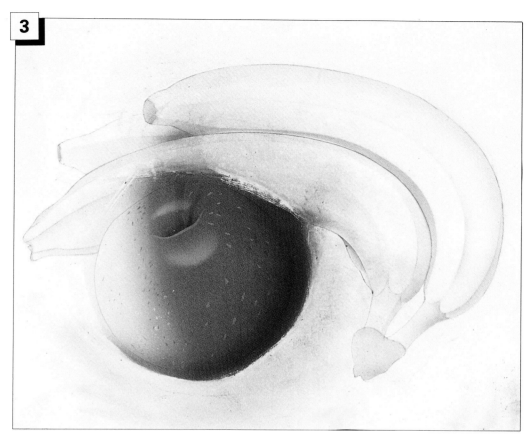

3 With the apple once again unmasked, except for the stalk, and the banana mask back in place, red and yellow can be sprayed in using gouache. The red, in this case, is vermilion deep sprayed flat, but vignetting off rapidly on the left side. The light monochrome wash will show through to add form, which can be enhanced later. The highlight is added with white gouache sprayed through another acetate loose mask. The yellow side of the apple is sprayed with a mixture of cadmium yellow and brilliant green, carefully vignetting back into red. The same mixture lightly sprayed through a prepared loose mask will add the characteristic spots marking an apple.

4

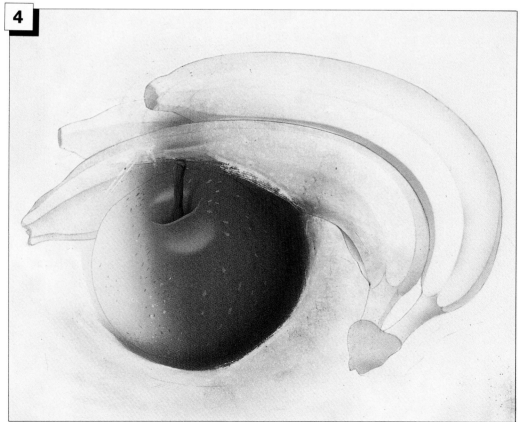

4 The final stage of work on the apple, for now, is to enhance the shadow by adding ivory black to the vermilion mixture, and working this in a freehand fashion down the right-hand side, until the correct depth is achieved. Then the mask can be removed from the apple stalk, and this detail added using Vandyke brown sprayed through the acetate mask.

5 A paper mask, slightly smaller than the apple image, is laid down for protection before the film mask is replaced over it, adhering only to the edges of the image. Then the masking from the bananas is removed. These are sprayed all over in a flat yellow gouache mixed from cadmium lemon with a touch of brilliant green.

6 Detailing can now be added to each of the three bananas using separate acetate masks. A little more green added to the yellow mixture is sprayed onto the edges of the bananas first, and then white highlights are added over the top of these with another mask. Vandyke brown added to the mixture completes most of the detailing when sprayed onto the stalks and ends, as well as into the shadows of each banana.

7

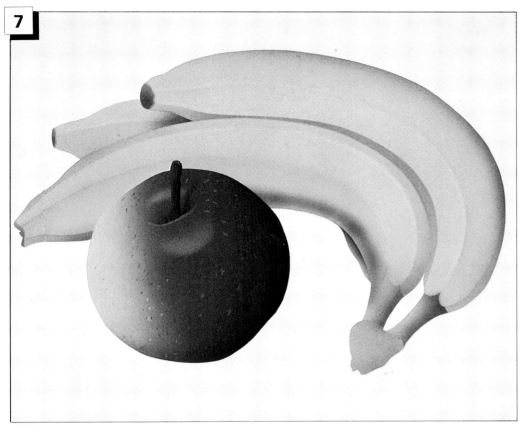

7 At this stage all of the masking is removed and the work is considered.

8

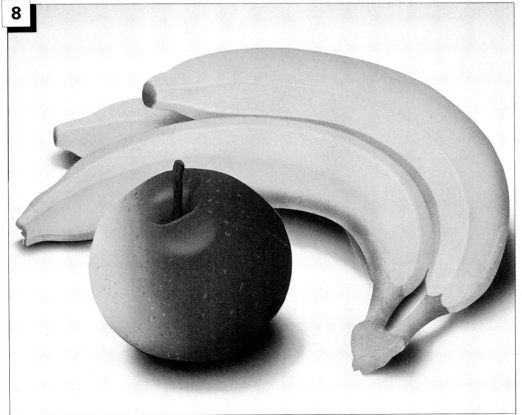

8 A shadow to 'ground' the fruit and a simple background vignette are added to give the picture greater depth and solidity. These are sprayed in using a mixture of black and blue inks diluted with water. The apple and bananas are masked with film, while an acetate mask held a little way above the board helps create a soft shadow underneath the fruit.

With the final mask removed, fine details can be added with a sable brush and gouache, while the apple highlights can be enhanced a little with white gouache sprayed freehand (see page 55).

HARVEST Brett Breckon

*While airbrushing is often associated with technical
or mechanical subjects, this painting proves that
natural forms can be equally successful subjects for
the medium, provided your approach and handling
is right.*

Most airbrush artists working in graphic or advertising fields will at some stage be asked to add sparkle to a piece of typography, usually a logo or other titling device. By and large the request will be for the lettering to appear metallic, both chrome and gold being popular finishes. This project will give you a step-by-step procedure for turning a plain typeface into a lively, three-dimensional logo.

The materials you will need are much the same as you have been using. Inks are demonstrated here since their transparency does not obscure the black keyline used as a base. However, if you prefer gouache, as many artists do, you can work up a similar illustration without a keyline, adding it and the drop shadow last of all. A technical pen will be required.

1 Choose a simple typeface constructed of straight lines and part circles. Create the logo and enlarge it to a suitable size – about 3 in (7.5 cm) high. Trace and transfer the logo to art board. Using a technical pen, ruler and templates, ink in the keyline and drop shadow. Cover the lettering with mall masking film. To create a raised surface to the letters, draw a border within each letter onto the film and cut out the central area.

2 Create a horizon line across the centre of the letters. Cover with tracing paper and draw a double line for the horizon, distorting it upward at the edge of each letter. Cover the tracing paper with masking film, remove from the artwork and cut out the horizon. Hold the loose mask to the artwork, and airbrush black along the horizon line, creating a soft but distinct edge.

3 When the black horizon line is created, remove the lower part of the loose mask and vignette down with red ink.

4 Remove the loose mask completely and add the second vignette, starting with blue at the top edge of the letters and gradually fading out to white to blend with the light touch of red just above the horizon line. By this stage the eventual success of the piece should be becoming apparent, but beware of rushing as the final steps will require a great deal of patience.

5 Replace all the film masks from the centres of the letters, and cut the film around the extreme edge of the letters, keeping to the keyline, and diagonals across each corner of the chamfered border. Remove the bottom edge of each letter, this will be the most shaded portion and therefore the darkest. Spray in the shadow, making sure not to make it black or it will be lost against the keyline. Next remove the side edges, leaving the top edges still masked, and spray in a blue on the right and scarlet on the left of each letter, vignetting them slightly for effect. Obviously, the curved sides of letters will have full vignette from dark to highlight and should be treated carefully.

6 When the ink is dry, lay masking film over the whole area and carefully cut around the lettering and border. Remove the film from the background area, remembering to take out any pieces in the centres of letters. The background can then be vignetted from a black, through blue, and then finally using scarlet over the blue to achieve the glow around the letters. When dry, all the masking can be removed to reveal your finished artwork.

CONTROL DATA – QUALITY

Brett Breckon

The illustration shown here is an example of airbrushed lettering in a graphic context. The painting, done in gouache, was produced for a large computer software company. The brief to the artist asked for the word 'Quality' to be created from an indeterminate but silicon-like substance, while the figure had to be dressed in the special protective clothing worn in the company's 'clean rooms'. Loose masking was used extensively to create the creases and sheen in the white work clothes, mask and hat, while fine brushwork completed the facial features.

P/R/O/J/E/C/T 3/: S/C/A/L/E F/O/R R/E/P/R/O/D/U/C/T/I/O/N

When you are thinking about an illustration, at some stage you are going to have to decide on the size of the finished artwork. There are several limiting factors involved in this decision, including time available and cost, but when the work is going to be used in reproduction, consideration has to be given to what size the printed version will be.

Most illustrators decide that working 'twice-up', or 'one-and-a-half times up' suits them best. This refers to the ratio of original to printed size, twice-up being literally twice the linear size so that a 10×8 in (25×20 cm) illustration is actually drawn and painted to 20×16 in (50×40 cm). The ratios can also be referred to as a percentage of the final size – 200%, 300%, 150%. The reduction to the printed size helps the illustrator since it compresses detail, hides tiny faults, and generally condenses the image to a more uniform whole. In commercial work this is essential, even though artistically it is perhaps not totally ethical. The time scale involved often leaves no times for tortuous attention to every minute detail in a picture, so by working in large bold strokes the marks become details under reduction.

Some illustrators stay closer to a fine art ethic, and work as near to the size of reproduction as possible, so that all of their marks can be read as essential parts of the whole. Working to the identical dimensions as the reproduction is called 'S/S' or 'same-size', and can also be shown as '100%'.

What all this means to you while your style of work evolves, is that you must be aware of size, and be prepared to try working at different scales until experienced enough to know what to put in and what to leave out as the situation requires.

RIGHT: *The two examples of a telephone handset reproduced here show that only half the work needs to be done if the final reduction is to be half size, while the visual quality remains almost the same.*

P/R/O/J/E/C/T 4/: S/Y/N/T/H/E/T/I/C/S

The suitability of the airbrush to render synthetic surfaces leads to its wide use in the graphics and advertising fields where, for the purpose of promotion, a product is often illustrated rather than photographed. This makes it possible to glamorize the subject, or set it in an artificial or surreal context, to attract the eye and arouse interest in a way that a straightforward product shot could not.

This project suggests just such an application. The viewer is caught by the apparent reality of what is after all an unlikely situation, and then before the realization dawns that it is a clever illustration, the image has done its job. Beyond that, of course, the illustration still arouses interest because of its attention to detail which makes the robot hand seem feasible, if not real.

This is how the illustration is approached.

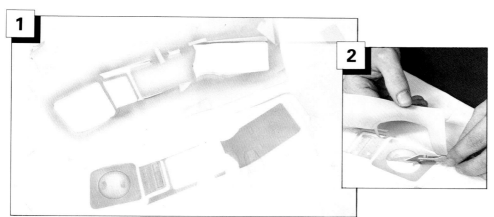

1 and **2** After completing the drawing, only the outline of the separate details are traced down. The telephone area is masked with matt film and then the moulding lines and reflection edges are traced onto the film. The dark green areas are removed first and sprayed in a flat colour. Then the lighter areas are removed and sprayed. The soft edges of the earpiece recess are created by making a loose mask and fixing it in place with a loop of masking tape.

3 and **4** The dark shadow down the side of the telephone is masked and sprayed next, and an ellipse template is used to apply tone to the ear recess. A fixed mask is cut for the black of the button panel and mouth and ear slots, and the colour sprayed over.

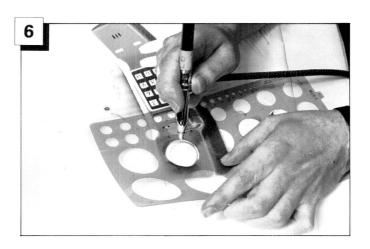

5 With the telephone virtually complete, the decision about whether to detail it at this point or later should be taken now. In this case, since the robot hand is being treated separately, the details of highlights, button numbers, small reflections and printing are all treated at this stage with fine sable brushwork.

6 The chromium hand can be treated with a single fixed film mask, and several loose masks to create reflections. The order of attack is to work from dark to light, putting in the horizon reflections and the reflection of the telephone before adding the light blue which gives the hand that cold robotic look. The extreme edges of details remain in light anticipation of the intended dark background in final reproduction.

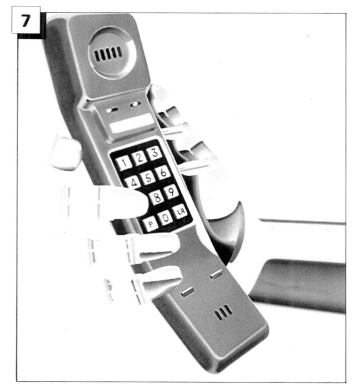

7, 8 and **9** The details of the servo-units in the fingers, and the black rubber flexible wrist joint are added with care since the finished illustration relies on such detail to appear feasible. Final detailing of joints, panel line, servo cables and reflections are added by hand with sable brushes, and the shadows of the fingers cast onto the telephone are lightly sprayed through a mask.

9

As almost any material that is a solid or partial barrier to the colour sprayed from your airbrush can be used as a mask, there is literally no limit to the number of special masking effects you can try.

Some will give results that will be used every day, while others will merely add to your experience. Eventually, the ways and means of achieving any finish you require will come as second nature.

Some suggestions have already been made in this book as to types of materials commonly used for preparing quick loose masks. Here are a few more ideas and examples that may be useful in themselves, and which will hopefully encourage you to experiment with ideas and materials of your own.

FISH SCALES

1 This simple technique to produce a clever overlapping fish scale texture can be achieved by making an acetate or card mask with a row of semi-circles meeting on a straight line running through their centres.

2 Holding this mask down to the board, a light spray is blown over forming a vignette, darkest in the curved 'Vs' between the semi-circles, and fading out just at the apex of their curves.

3 The mask is then pulled down and shifted one circle radius across so that the previous silhouette just touches the circle tops, and another row is blown in.

4 This sequence can be repeated until the area required is covered.

RIGHT: *This book jacket illustration shows the fish-scale technique used effectively to enhance the 'Big Fish' typography. The fine wood grain and carved detail on the gun handle were hand painted after the basic wood tone and shading were airbrushed in.*

STARBURST TECHNIQUE

Another useful loose mask technique to master is for adding a glossy 'starburst' to a highlight, suggesting dazzle or glamour. If you are adding several starbursts to one illustration you should keep them all at the same angle as each other.

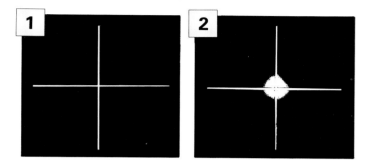

1 This can be achieved simply by cutting two thin slits crossing at right angles to each other in thin, dark card. The slits should each be about 1/10 in (1 mm) wide and 3 in (8 cm) long.

2 Place the intersection of the slits on your artwork directly over the point of highlight and spray white gouache through while holding the mask firmly down.

3 A final finishing free-hand dot of white can be sprayed into the centre of the starburst once the mask has been removed.

GAUZE AND MESH

There are many gauzes and meshes which can be used to spray through. You can also try the following. Stipple masking fluid through a fine mesh with a stiff hogs-hair or bristle brush. Remove the mesh and spray over the resulting pattern when the masking fluid has dried. Upon removal of the dried mask a textured positive of the mesh will result.

DRY TRANSFER LETTERING

Instant rub-down lettering will also form a mask, although it, like masking fluid, is best used on virgin board, not on previously applied paint. After spraying, the applied dry transfer can be removed by gently picking away with curls of masking tape and then, if necessary, a lighter transparent tone can be sprayed across the whole artwork to deaden the stark white board.

ABOVE: *In this illustration of pool balls a certain economy of masking has been observed, although without detriment to the finished product, which has a very photographic finish. One fixed mask has given the balls crisp, precise edges against the baize surface of the table, which has been built up in a spatter fashion. Then, with the background masked out, all the* *detail on the balls was achieved with loose masks, using ellipse and circle templates, and a straightedge to create the yellow stripe on the nine ball. Notice how the blue, red and purple balls all use the same loose mask to create the angular reflection. All in all, this is a clever, well thought out illustration, where 'using least to achieve most' might well have been the maxim.*

P/R/O/J/E/C/T 6/:
T/H/E I/M/P/O/R/T/A/N/C/E
O/F P/R/E/L/I/M/I/N/A/R/Y
W/O/R/K

Part of the process of producing an illustration is the preparation of visuals. There are two reasons for this. Firstly, you may have to work out the concept of the image before committing yourself to the final piece of work, and secondly, you may need to convince a client that your proposal for the work is sound and usable.

Almost all illustrators produce visuals, roughs or scamps (as they are alternatively known) at some stage in the process of producing an airbrushed painting, and these vary greatly in complexity and thoroughness. Some go to the lengths of preparing a fully airbrushed visual, either because the client needs to see the technique at this stage, or because the process suggests methods of progressing on the final piece. Other artists keep preliminary work to a minimum, just roughing out colour areas with a marker before proceeding. It can be a mark of a client's confidence should an illustrator be allowed to proceed on only a thumbnail sketch; this is most likely to happen in tried and trusted partnerships.

The visual and finished artwork shown here were for a thriller book jacket. The publisher's art director had expressed his ideas for a simple design, and asked for a visual to assess how successful the image was likely to be. For the illustrator it gave the opportunity to work out not only the component parts of the piece and their physical relationship, but also the colour variations within those components. There was no need for a fully airbrushed visual; anyway, time and budget made this impossible. Instead, once the brief had been received, a few sketches were produced to try out variations of composition and form. From these the art director made his recommendations and suggestions which led to the colour visual. This received client approval and the go-ahead was given to produce the final artwork.

BELOW: Terminal, *Brett Breckon. A colour visual was first executed* LEFT *and presented for client approval.*

These two paintings are examples of individual airbrush styles that show how similar subjects can be treated in wholly different manners to achieve different end results.

With Ean Taylor's CADILLAC there is a strong graphic unity in the image which has been amplified by the stylized technique. Each shape, each reflection is reduced to a purer, simpler form by the extensive use of hard masking and vibrant colour. Inks were used for their transparency to help heighten the whole effect and lift a realistic situation into the hyper-realistic, or even surrealistic. Because the reality was already there, this transformation into something outside of that reality was necessary to make an interesting, enjoyable and worthwhile image.

On the other hand, Brett Breckon's SHE'S A MAID IN HEAVEN, HE'S A KNIGHT ON THE TILES, *required a more subdued approach so that a surrealistic situation could be made believable. Gouache is the medium used, with hard masking being* complemented by loose masking and freehand work. The reflections in the chrome were considered, and then painted by hand after the simple blue was airbrushed in. Detailing the receding chess board squares reflected into the underside of the bumpers helps to reinforce the feeling that everything is real. Minute details were added to the figures with fine sable brushwork and every attempt was made to give the viewer fragments of plausibility to cling to in a surreal context.

P/R/O/J/E/C/T 7:
T/E/X/T/U/R/E

All of the exercises and projects that have been illustrated in this book were designed to give you the broadest possible introduction to airbrushing. If you have completed the lessons or used their instructions on work of your own, then you will have tried out most, if not all, of the methods that the best airbrush artists use. That being the case, it is a good idea to try a full-blown illustration to test both your technical ability and artistic flair.

This final step-by-step project has one or two new suggestions to add to your repertoire, while also requiring a high degree of finish and airbrushing know-how to execute successfully. It is, like Project 1, a still-life, but this time explores the textures of chrome and silk – two contrasting materials that can be rendered very satisfactorily with an airbrush.

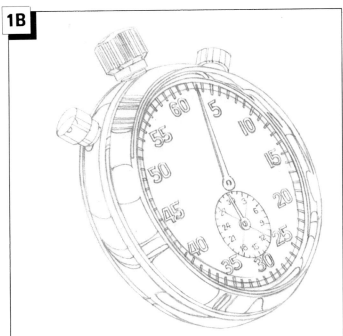

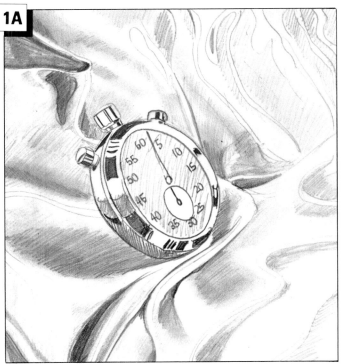

1 The first stage, as always, is to gather together reference material, either photographic or, in this case, real life, and to prepare the piece by working up sketches, visuals and drawings. While there are many professional illustrators who would rather leave some of the experimenting, either with colour, form or texture, to the final piece of work, others resolve the image in their minds and on paper almost completely before committing themselves to the final piece. You have to decide for yourself how much preliminary work you require before tackling the finished artwork. It is a decision you must base on confidence and experience.

Here the artist has finalized the basic form and design of the illustration in one of his preliminary sketches **1A**, and from this an accurate trace of the chromium-plated stopwatch can be worked up **1B**.

2 The next step is to transfer this to art board, cover the image with masking film and cut around the various shapes and components before beginning to spray. The raised band around the body of the watch is sprayed first using a mixture of black and cobalt blue inks diluted with water. After each section is sprayed, its protective mask is replaced and an adjacent area treated. The two faces of the raised band have alternating simple vignettes of the colour blown into them to achieve the illusion of the form. Next, with this area re-masked, the broader areas of chrome are revealed ready for spraying.

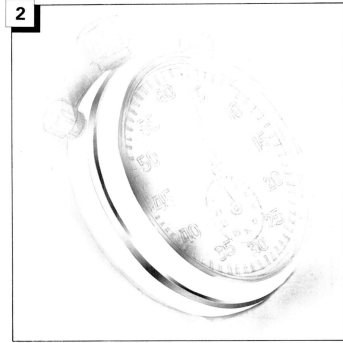

3

3 Loose masks cut from acetate sheet and hand-held in place are used to create the reflections in these sections. The successful portrayal of chomium depends upon both hard-edged reflections and soft vignettes, with stark contrasts between highlights and shadows.

4

4 Detailing the buttons of the watch, and the inner edge of the chrome body requires careful use of masking film and scalpel, as well as the astute use of loose masking. This is where consideration and preliminary work both pay off. If ever you are in doubt about a mark you are about to make, it is wise to stop and consider it first. If necessary go back to your visual to find the answer before making any marks on your artwork that could be disastrous.

5

5 By now the stopwatch body is looking fine, if a little monochrome. Colour will be added after the background is completed, so that the correct reflected colour may be applied. The watch face is treated next. This entails masking off the figures, hand and smaller dial, which is sprayed separately to a shiny finish using loose masks. A solid black goes down onto the face, lightening on the left side where the glass will be suggested by a highlight.

6

6 The watch glass highlight is added using a loose acetate mask, and with white gouache in the airbrush. All the masking for the figures is then removed and the effect of the whole thing considered.

7 At this stage all the work on the stopwatch is halted, since only detailing and reflected colour remains to be done. The background mask is removed now, and the watch masked off, with a thin paper patch protecting the central area from adhesion by the film.

8 To avoid unwanted pencil lines showing through the light background details, the highlight lines are drawn onto the matt masking film after it is laid in place. These are then cut and unwanted areas removed. A flat overall covering of the body colour, a mixture of scarlet and Mars red inks, is then applied.

9

9 Using a greater concentration of the same colours the folded forms of the silk are described with both freehand marks and loose acetate masks, where an edge is created by a fold. This is where confidence and experience with the airbrush really begins to show, for at this stage it is vital to constantly check back to the reference material.

10

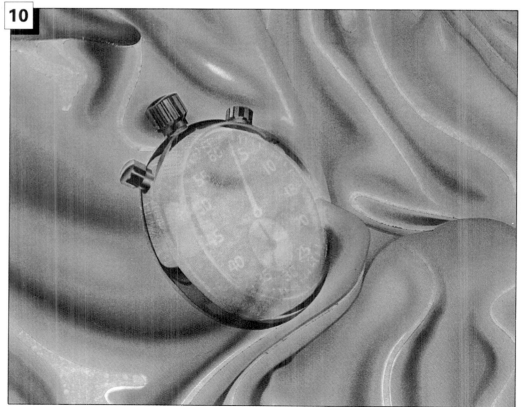

10 A little black ink added to the mixture and sprayed into the shadow areas starts to give the material its characteristic lustre. The same loose masks are re-used until the correct depth of colour has been achieved.

11 The masks are now removed from the highlights. The edges the fixed masks have created are obviously too crisp for the satin sheen the material needs, and so the edges are softened by careful use of a typist's erasing pencil. These are hard-compound erasers that can be sharpened to a very fine point.

12 Finally a diluted mixture of the silk colour is used to soften off the highlights once more, and individual attention is paid to creases and folds in the materials where necessary.

13 Now, with the background completed, the watch is exposed again, and the warm silk colour is blown into the chromium reflections using acetate masks. Final detailing to the watch face completes the illustration.

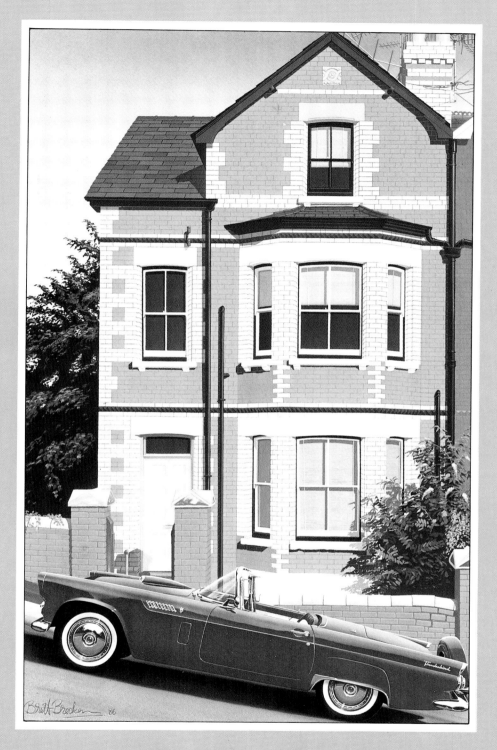

PARTING SHOT Brett Breckon

There is no fixed modus operandi *for airbrush users, as this painting shows when compared with the previous project. Here the airbrush has been used subtly in conjunction with brushapplied paint. While the car might be a traditional airbrush subject, in fact only its red body, the whitewall tyres, and the windshield reflections have been applied this way. The chrome – perhaps THE traditional airbrush subject – is hand painted in great detail.*

It could be said that airbrushing and technical illustration were made for each other; certainly they were closely allied long before the airbrush finally came into its own as a versatile painting implement. But what is technical illustration? Where does it end and the more esoteric forms of illustration begin? Should you be reading this section if you have no idea how a turbo charged racing engine looks from within; and would you rather climb Everest than attempt a cutaway drawing of even a lump of butter?

Well, the answer to the last question is yes, because while the disciplines of technical drawing may be totally removed from your work, there are many occasions when you will produce a technical answer to an illustration question. The two often do overlap, and the more artistic illustrator can learn a lot from the craft of the airbrush technician.

P/R/O/F/I/L/E I/L/L/U/S/T/R/A/T/I/O/N

This project, producing a 'profile' illustration of a car, is a technical illustration in that it is educational and dissolves doubt about details of the car's external features.

The purpose of this illustration is to provide precise visual information in a clear way. A photograph would have distracting information – background and foreground, reflections that distort or hide details – whereas an illustration can be pristine and clear in its details. This can involve referring to many photographs for details, while using just one to provide the basic form.

The illustration was built up as follows.

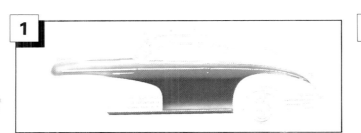

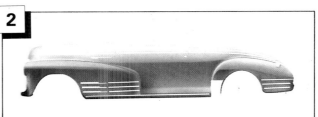

1 From reference material an accurate line drawing was made. This was traced and transferred to art board. The first fixed mask was prepared to expose the side panels and hood, and these sprayed with inks, vignetting out along the rounded hood side and at the base of the door. A loose mask was cut to create a reflected horizon.

2 The fenders were masked and sprayed next, and loose masking was used to create a corresponding horizon reflection in them. Thorough research is necessary here, since the horizon reflection has to 'sit' correctly to accurately describe the panelling contours.

3 The roof, window surrounds and rear light fairing were treated next using loose masking, each receiving individual attention for colour consistency.

4 and **5** With the interior detail, the whole illustration is beginning to come alive. The side windows have a soft reflection across them created with a cut paper mask. Notice the attention to correct shadowing on the whitewall tyres, achieved with careful freehand work and the use of a circle template as a loose mask.

6 and **7** The wheels are treated with two fixed masks, one for the chrome hub cap, which itself has soft-masked simplified reflections in it, and the other for the steel wheel surround.

8 The final stage is to finish off details. For example, chrome fenders and side trims received simple airbrushing in blue, before being detailed and shadowed with a very fine brush and paint.

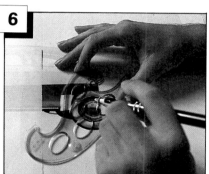

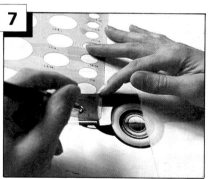

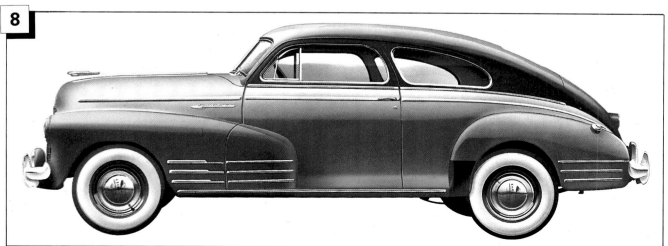

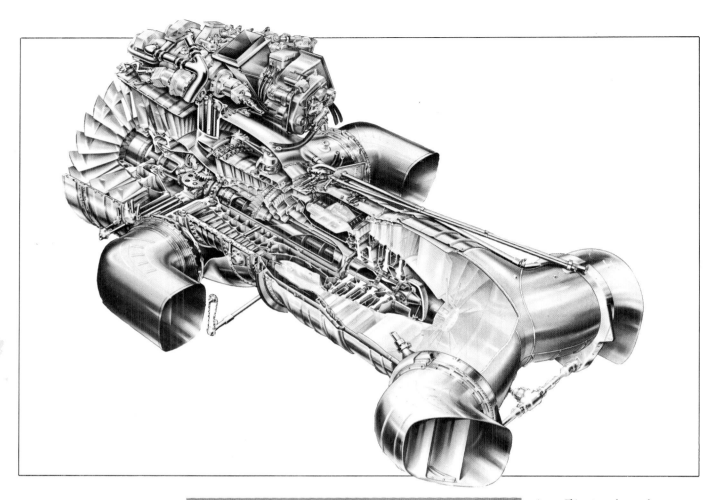

ABOVE: *This extremely complex airbrush illustration of a Rolls Royce engine was probably commissioned as an information exercise to attract prospective clients.*

C/U/T/A/W/A/Y D/R/A/W/I/N/G

The clever use of cutaway drawings is one of the hallmarks of the technical illustrator. The technique has been devised so that both the external form of a machine or device can be portrayed, with the insides or workings opened up to view by removing portions of outer layers. In this way, each important component can be seen *in situ*, clearly showing its function and relationship to other components.

The heights to which the technique has been taken are quite phenomenal, with drawings often being on vast scales, opening up the workings of such complex machines as jet aero-engines, where each of the thousands of fan blades is individually drawn and rendered along with all the ancillary piping, gearing and sub-systems that make the engine work. This level of achievement requires years of apprenticeship before you would be allowed to undertake even a tiny aspect of a whole job, which would in any case be executed by a team of designers and technicians, each handling a particular part of the drawing.

The other end of the scale can, however, be approached by the beginner. However, some training in technical drawing is helpful in order to understand the various methods of constructing, for example, representing isometric views of objects, or taking information and measurements from engineer's drawings or from the objects themselves.

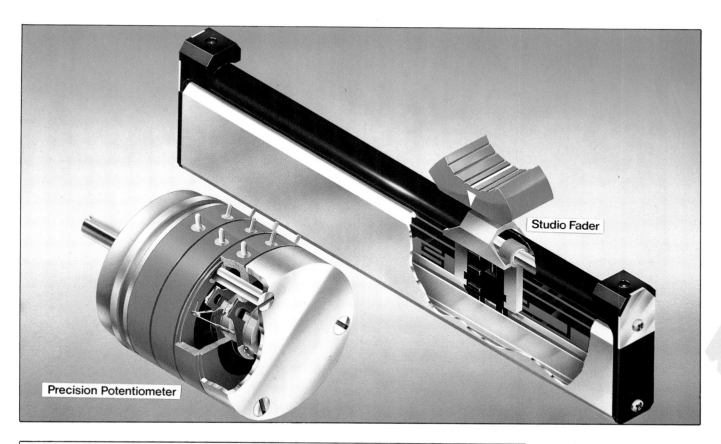

Studio Fader

Precision Potentiometer

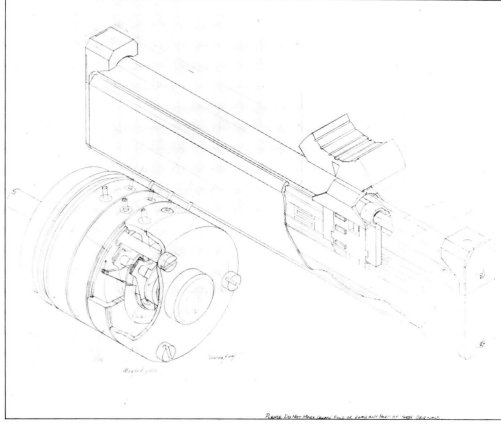

PLEASE DO NOT MARK CREASE FOLD OR FRAME ANY PART OF THESE ORIGINALS

ABOVE: *These potentiometers are shown in a cutaway style and were drawn in isometric projection, using as reference both the original engineer's drawings and examples of the devices themselves, which were dismantled and studied for function, dimensions and structure. The drawings* LEFT *show how construction lines were used to build up and encase the form of each major feature, before the final outline could be drawn in more heavily. The actual segments to be cut away had to be carefully chosen to make all the relevant information about external and internal components clear and definitive. In some areas a linear cut through the casing was used to show the profile inside that section, while an uneven, broken edge was used in other areas to leave the viewer in no doubt that in reality the casing continues and the cutaway is not a part of the project.*

When the drawings had been completed and had received client approval, the relevant details were traced off and transferred to art board. They were then airbrushed in using gouache, with details being added by hand with fine sable paintbrushes. The background vignettes were added last of all.

HENLEY

ABOVE: *This dramatic cutaway illustration of a suspension unit was airbrushed onto a solid black background so that the light metallic parts stood out in stark contrast giving them a higher visibility than they would have on a more usual white background. The opacity of gouache was used to build up the solid whites over the black, and then the subtle hues of watercolour were airbrushed over to add colour to the image, with their transparency making it possible to fade the tyre and other less essential parts into the background.*

K/E/Y/L/I/N/E
I/L/L/U/S/T/R/A/T/I/O/N

Using a keyline as the basis of an illustration is very useful when details need to be brought to the fore and emphasized, and where a more realistic approach would be likely to distract the viewer with inconsequential information. Also as a graphic technique a keyline can add definition to a subject, making it visually more interesting than a photograph would do.

The cover for the 'HTV Programme Review 1986' was first drawn as three separate elements. The brief called for the whole image to be graphically believable without necessarily being technically correct. Therefore, the keyline approach was used to make the video-tape machines appear less cluttered than they actually are, clarifying

details by outlining them, while omitting unnecessary and therefore distracting details.

Once the three elements had been drawn, and their relative sizes and positions fixed, they were traced off and transferred to art board. The keyline was then inked in with technical pens, with great care taken not to touch the board with hands while this major operation was undertaken.

Working on small sections at a time, with all other areas covered with paper, fixed masks were then cut. Simple vignettes were air-brushed with inks maintaining a stylized image.

When all the airbrushing was completed, gouache was used to add small details, highlighting on features and panel edges, and the small shadows beneath switches, knobs, etc.

The finished printed version appeared with a strong blue back-ground and red connecting arrows, which were created as separate artwork and then dropped in by the printer.

LEFT: *The illustration in the form that it left the artist, and* ABOVE *as it appeared in print, with the addition of keylines.*

The more complex keyline illustration of a Porsche racing car was produced as two separate pieces of artwork, one containing all the colour areas, the other the keyline drawing. This was made possible by producing the keyline drawing and having it photographically reproduced on clear film as a film positive. A second sheet of film was positioned over this and held in place while the colour was sprayed onto it, being very careful with the masking film which was cut to the contours of the drawing below.

The internal details of the car were coloured first and made to appear solid, while the body was lightly sprayed over in a transparent 'ghosting' fashion so that all the relevant detail showed through clearly. Finally, the sponsor's badges and decals were coloured solidly.

After all the colouring was completed, and for reproduction purposes the keyline was removed from beneath the coloured artwork and placed over it to form an overlay to tie all the details together.

The technical illustrator is often called upon to produce a factual, lifelike rendering of a product that does not yet exist. It is at this time that the ability to read and understand an engineer's drawings can really be an asset, since these are sometimes the only form that the product yet takes. In themselves, they are insufficient to convince other people. But with an airbrush, which can realistically render most of the materials used in manufacture, a believable representation can be made, especially if cutaway or ghosting techniques are used. Thus, financial backers or prospective customers are given something more substantial than the clinical and complex plans and elevations of an engineer's drawings.

ABOVE: *The keyline illustration of a Porsche 934 was produced from two pieces of artwork, one to show the colour work* TOP LEFT *and the other the keyline* BOTTOM LEFT.

BELOW: *The brief for this illustration of the proposed 'AWACS' (Airborne Warning And Control System) aircraft, based on a Boeing 737, demanded an anonymous colour scheme for the aircraft and, to add greater realism, a pictorial background had to be incorporated.*

PHOTO-RETOUCHING

5

Long before airbrushing became accepted as a popular and widespread art technique, there was a small army of airbrush technicians quietly going about the work of retouching photographs. The ironic fact is that throughout its history photography has been plagued by the shortcomings and unpredictability of reality. Methods have always been needed to enhance the truth in a medium that – ostensibly – could not lie.

From very early on it was discovered that airbrushing was the most sympathetic way to improve photographic images, and today it still remains irreplaceable, even though photography and photographic techniques have moved into the computer age, where machines can disassemble and reassemble seamless images from various photographic sources.

Airbrush photo-retouching is a highly skilled field, with an equally wide variety of applications. It is dominated by the work done in the advertising industry where almost every photographic image produced has been treated by a retoucher, the best of whom have the ability to manipulate images on print, film, negative and transparency.

Such techniques are far beyond the beginner, and the realm of this book. However, for those of you with an interest in, or an enthusiasm for the subject and its possibilities, the following chapter serves as an introduction.

Basically, retouching encompasses the addition or removal of visual information to or from a photograph, and also includes photomontage where images from two or more sources are brought together and unified into one. The ultimate criterion for all retouching work is that it should remain invisible in itself, so that the whole image seems 'real' to the viewer, however bizarre the retouching has made that reality. This calls for an intensely clinical approach to the work, and precise control over technical skills.

The exercises and examples in this section are designed to provide a foundation, and as such they are quite simple and practical, dealing only with basic retouching requirements.

ABOVE: *The airbrush is used in photo-retouching for a variety of effects: to create new areas of visual information or to simply hide a mark or join, as in this example of montage, where a photograph of the actor Jack Nicholson has been inserted in a 1923 group photograph.*

LEFT: *This example of commercial retouching shows how, working directly onto a colour print, a new colour scheme and insignia can be inserted onto an existing image.*

BELOW: *This photomontage by Richard Manning was constructed from four separate images, which were pieced together. A bow wave was then airbrushed in and a sepia print of the whole image made. This was then coloured with photographic water-based dyes, using both airbrush and paintbrush.*

Black and white photographs are used to demonstrate the art since this is one area of retouching still dominated by the airbrush. Most colour-retouching work is now performed by laboratories, using expensive and complex processing procedures, which cannot be explained or imitated here. Also, black and white work is cheaper for you to experiment on.

One area of colour work that will be looked at here is the hand-tinting of monochrome prints. Here, at least, the selectiveness of the artist's eye has not yet been replaced by the workings of a machine, and very individual statements, as well as wonderfully subtle images, can be created with the deft use of airbrushed transparent colours over photographic originals.

R/E/T/O/U/C/H/I/N/G M/A/T/E/R/I/A/L/S

Most of the techniques and methods of air brush illustration that have been dealt with earlier can be utilized in retouching photographs by hand and, similarly, many of the materials used are also applicable to both fields of work. However, to complement your original materials list, there are a few specialized items which may be of use to you when attempting these exercises.

MEDIA

For the most part, black and white photo-retouching can be undertaken using gouache and tube watercolour paints. The opacity of the gouache medium is especially important since retouching usually requires obscuring visual information in a print to allow for the positioning of new information over it. Use permanent white and jet black colours, complemented with Vandyke brown, which is used in tiny amounts to warm the greys to match the tones of prints. Using just black and white paint to mix the greys will create blue-greys that do not sit well on the photograph and produce an unconvincing result. There are special retouching paints available in tubes and in a

range of greys, in matt or gloss finish, to match the paper you are working on; but while these might seem convenient they are not essential. It is cheaper, and more comfortable for the beginner to stay with familiar media.

Transparent colours, such as the watercolours and inks described in previous chapters, are useful when the photographic image is to be enhanced by retouching, and not completely obscured, as in hand-tinting.

MASKING

Fixed film masking is the mainstay of most airbrush retouching, and it is applied in the same manner as in illustration work. However, even greater care must be taken in the cutting operation; it is harder to conceal a scored photographic surface and greater precision is required if the photographic qualities are to be matched.

Liquid masking is still favoured by many for very small and complex shapes, although its opacity does make it inconvenient when trying to match an area of tone.

Loose masks can be created in the same way as for illustrations. Photography also has the advantage of being able to provide you with duplicate prints of the image you are working on. These can be

Background treatments *Altering a background can save a poorly composed picture. The original photograph* FAR LEFT *was marred by a cluttered, unattractive background.*

White background *A tracing paper mask, reinforced with film, was held in place and process white sprayed from side to side.*

Vignetted background *A mid-grey tone was used to obliterate the background detail, and a second, darker tone applied in a vignette.*

Halo *An oval shape was cut from cardboard, the figure masked off and the background sprayed in a dark tone. The mask was removed and the cut-out oval placed over the print, supported on coins. A light spray was then applied from the centre of the cardboard to soften the hard-masked edge.*

cut to provide loose masks with exact outlines, which can be removed to allow accurate tonal matching and examination of detail.

PHOTOGRAPHIC PAPERS

When ordering your photographs for retouching, bear in mind the paper on which the print will be made. There are two suitable types – bromide and resin coated – and these come in matt, gloss or satin finishes. By and large it is the matt finish that is most suitable, since an applied medium invariably dries matt and so on this surface a clearer indication of the success of a piece of retouching can be seen.

Whichever type of paper you choose, it should be securely mounted onto a stiff, flat board. Bromide papers can be dry mounted, whereas resin coated stock, which is melted by heat, should be mounted using aerosol-applied glue, which has the added advantage of being impermanent. This means that the photograph can be stripped away from the support once the retouching work is complete, leaving it flexible and versatile.

One disadvantage of resin-coated papers is that paint does not adhere to them very well when applied by brush, and an overly wet paintbrush will damage areas already painted with an airbrush. The solution to this problem is to make sure that when painting over airbrush work your paint is of a thick creamy, consistency. If adding a paintbrush mark to un-retouched paper, spray the area first with a solution of gum arabic which will provide a thin film base to support the paint.

Always degrease and clean photographic paper with lighter fluid before commencing work, as you do with illustration board, but be very careful not to rub too hard with the cotton wool, because even this will leave tiny scratches in the delicate surface.

T/H/E W/O/R/K O/F T/H/E R/E/T/O/U/C/H/E/R

There are many misconceptions as to what 'retouching' means; the most common belief being that a photograph is retouched to hide the fact that it is not a 'good' photograph to begin with.

The truth is that almost every photograph published has received some attention at the hands of a retoucher, whether it be a simple case of 'spotting out', or the removal of a portion of image to allow for the addition of a new element. It is a testament to the retoucher's art that most of this work goes unnoticed, even though large areas of magazine and billboard advertisements have often been altered between photography and final printing. The low opinion some people have for the art usually comes from seeing blatant examples of retouching that are obviously flawed. On the other hand, an apparently 'perfect' product shot in an advertisement, for example, is assumed to be a straightforward photograph, even though it may be heavily retouched.

In fact, the product shot is a particularly good example of where retouching frequently needs to be employed. When photographing something like a bottle of whisky, lighting will be used to make the bottle and its contents as attractive as possible. This can lead to unwanted or unnecessary highlights and reflections which the retoucher will take out or obscure. Similarly, when details are enlarged, no matter how perfect the specimen that was photographed, flaws will emerge that need correction. And in shooting large objects or complex shapes, the lighting employed for the best shot will often be insufficient to lift every detail from the printed page, so small sections and areas in shadow can be heightened later in the retouching studio.

The photojournalist or editorial photographer makes other demands on the retoucher. Here, work is undertaken in totally different conditions to the studio photographer. The subjects are sometimes difficult to photograph, often unwilling to *be* photographed, and are usually recorded in a split second. This means that prints from in-the-field reportage are often blurred and unclear, or their subjects are lost in a sea of overwhelming background detail. On such occasions, simple and often quite crude work is done to lift important features within the picture, while care is taken not to distort the truth of what it carries. This is the most important principle in this kind of work – the aim here is to aid the reproduction of a photograph rather than alter what it has to say. Unfortunately, it is true to say that this process has been used for propagandist purposes, to alter the truth that people are allowed to see and read. Ethically, this is not an aspect of journalistic retouching that should be pursued.

ABOVE: *This example of photo-retouching shows how the process can be used to produce a flat, clean image, which sometimes eludes the abilities of the photographer alone. The studio shot* LEFT *did not achieve the desired definition of feature. The retoucher obliterated superfluous facial details and heightened the colouring of hair and eyes* ABOVE RIGHT *to produce the required dramatic book jacket design* RIGHT.

MONEY CAN'T BUY LOVE…IT *CAN* BUY PLEASURE

Her elderly husband's death leaves Jenny Townsend grief-stricken – but rich. And Jenny soon finds that a multi-million dollar fortune can buy almost everything.

To keep the money she has to obey her husband's dying wish: she must marry again, but only after she has tried many lovers.

Wildly rich, desperately alone and hungry for passion, Jenny has six months in which to experience every pleasure money can buy. Then – and only then – can she marry for love.

Don't miss Francesca Greer's other sensational novels:
FIRST FIRE
BRIGHT DAWN
also available in Sphere Books.

0 7221 4080 0   CONTEMPORARY ROMANCE

E/X/A/M/P/L/E 1/: P/R/I/N/T R/E/S/T/O/R/A/T/I/O/N

If you want to develop your skills as a retoucher, a very useful start is to rummage through old family photograph albums for damaged prints. Torn edges, creases, holes, fading, finger prints – all these can make a once cherished picture quite unusable except, that is, as an exercise in photograph restoration.

The first thing to do is to have the picture re-photographed and two or more enlarged prints made out of it. Never attempt to work directly onto a valuable original because if you do, and make an error, it may be lost forever.

Study the copy carefully and assess its qualities. Look at the graining, and the sharpness of focus to outlines. Tonal qualities which will need matching should also be examined, as well as details that need to be retained, or even heightened, in retouching.

The example shown here, of a young boy standing next to a cane chair, has certainly suffered over the years. The original print has lost the top right-hand corner, and has various scratches and tears. Outlines are blurred and often indistinct, making it quite obvious that loose masking would be essential, since hard-edged fixed masking would destroy the whole quality of the piece. The very grainy finish within the picture also calls for the use of lower than usual air pressures through the airbrush. The second copy of the print was made to provide accurate loose masks, and this was cut into its component parts. The retouching proceeds as follows.

STAGE 1: The whole of the right-hand side of the photograph is in need of attention. The areas of the boy's arm and hair that are missing, as well as the chair back, are first drawn onto the spare print. The now complete outline of both boy and chair is cut out to be used as a loose mask.

A tonal palette of greys is mixed using black and white gouache, with small amounts of Vandyke brown to warm the colours to match the photographic tones, and a dark grey was loaded into the airbrush. The missing top right corner of the image is sprayed, carefully manipulating the loose mask to maintain soft edges. In this way, the torn edge is obliterated before a lighter grey is blown back onto the print to match the original tone. The various scratches and tears lower down receive similar treatment, while all the time the light and shade falling on the background drape is matched as closely as possible.

STAGE 2: The second half of the loose mask is brought into use next to mend the torn areas of arm, hair and chair back. Again a darker tone is used to obliterate the tear, before lighter tones are blown in to match the original. A good deal of freehand work is possible with no masking at all since the soft-focus quality of the picture seems to require this. However, confidence and experience is required here, and the work should never be rushed.

At this stage the outline of the boy is strengthened slightly since in areas of the original it had faded so much that it had begun to merge with the background.

STAGE 3: The tear across the centre of the picture is dealt with next, largely freehand, working each section of chair, fabric, background, etc, separately.

The ringlets in the boy's hair are also detailed at this stage, matching as closely as possible those visible on the undamaged side of his head, using freehand strokes added over a darker base colour.

STAGE 4: The final stage is spotting out the remaining small tears, dust marks and hair-lines on the print with a fine sable brush. The whole image is to some extent affected by these, but to airbrush them all out would have meant covering so much of the print that the qualities inherent in the original would have been lost completely.

When all the retouching is complete the finished piece can be rephotographed and a final print made, which will unify all the tones of paint and print. A sepia print can then be made, recapturing the charm of the original.

E/X/A/M/P/L/E 2/: R/E/M/O/V/I/N/G B/A/C/K/G/R/O/U/N/D D/E/T/A/I/L

One of the most frequent requests from design companies is to remove background detail from a product shot, pick out small details lost or overlooked by the photographer and generally clean up and enhance the subject's appearance. The photographs requiring attention may be of anything from a small manufactured item, carefully shot in a studio and needing a little retouch work, to large industrial machines which have to be shot *in situ*, often in poor lighting conditions and in an unattractive environment.

Dropping a background out to white is a fairly simple process in itself, although depending upon the complexity of the subject cutting the mask can be tricky, and patience is required when building up a solid white. Trying to achieve this in one or two heavy passes of the airbrush should never be attempted, or else overly wet and uneven pools of paint will form, and upon drying they may crack or lift when masked over.

The method you should adopt is to cover the subject and any parts of the print required to be seen with masking film. If the background is largely of light tones anyway, and with no harsh contrasting lines, you can spray with white gouache immediately, building up a solid with light passes of the airbrush. Allow each coat to dry before spraying the next. If, however, the background has a lot of contrasting tones, as in this case with the factory yard, you will find it far easier to spray a mid-tone grey which will obliterate all details far more readily than white. Then, once the grey has dried flat, you can apply white, which will cover to an acceptable solid with relative ease.

Once you have removed the mask, and the subject is no longer cluttered with distracting details, it will be easier to judge the cleaning-up task ahead.

In the example shown, heavily shadowed areas beneath the platform and between the legs around the hydraulic gear were treated to lighten and define the details. The wheels and tyres were cleaned up and highlighted, as was the control panel. Other panels and parts were highlighted and shadowed with a fine sable brush and ruler to help define them and enhance the 'clean' look of the finished piece.

E/X/A/M/P/L/E 3/: R/E/S/C/U/I/N/G A P/H/O/T/O/G/R/A/P/H

Photographs may be passed on to the retoucher because they are quite inadequate to serve the task for which they were ordered. This can happen when a photographer has been given the wrong brief, was not supplied with all the information for the job, or was poorly art directed. Sometimes it is the clients who change their mind, and then photographs which were originally acceptable suddenly fall short of requirements – though time or budget make a re-shoot impossible. Whatever the reason, in cases like these the retoucher has to save the day. The main problem, then, is to assess the information available. This may involve intuitive interpretation of the

photograph, or a more thorough research of the subject in order to add details that are not evident but which are essential.

In this example a much-used rock drill has been photographed in such a way that details down the right-hand side are eclipsed by shadows, while on the left they are defeated by glaring highlights. Also, various changes have been stipulated such as making the rubber muffler black rather than white, drawing on a new chisel tip, and also obliterating the stand and background.

In work of this kind it helps to be well versed in the ways of retouching machines and problems can then be overcome by tried and tested answers. A good knowledge of nuts, bolts, jubilee clips and the like helps with the interpretation of scant details on poor photographs such as this. You should never begin working unless you have all the information needed to finish the job. Vagueness is not generally in keeping with the nature of photo-retouching, and air-brushing is not a lenient or forgiving process if you begin to fudge things while trying to work out a solution.

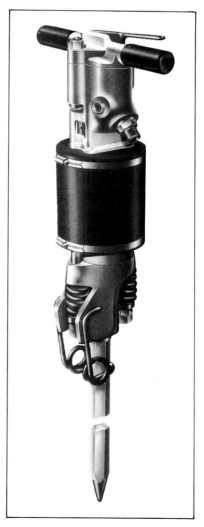

ABOVE: *The rather 'grainy' photograph of a rock drill* LEFT *was totally inadequate for the manufacturer's brochure. The retoucher removed the stand and background, clarified the detail and added the tip from reference material.*

E/X/A/M/P/L/E 4/:
P/H/O/T/O/M/O/N/T/A/G/E
A/N/D
H/A/N/D T/I/N/T/I/N/G

Photomontage is the process of taking images from two or more photographic sources and combining them to create a single new image. Historically, the technique has been used to great effect in propaganda works and for political comment, while the surreal possibilities have been exploited by artists and satirists to produce images of varying degrees of plausibility to either fool, astonish or amuse the viewer.

As far as the airbrush is concerned, its role is quite minimal in montage work, restricted in touching out joins that have remained visible in the final print. However, there is one area of montage work that throws open interesting and exciting possibilities for the airbrush user where the montage is coupled with hand tinting to create a whole new form of illustration, as shown in these two examples by the artist Simon Fell.

In the first, titled 'Industry Year', the images have been culled from picture library sources and then photocopied, sometimes several times at different sizes. These copies have been cut up to provide the raw material for the montage, which was assembled using spray glue. A great deal of attention was paid to maintaining correct perspectives in order that the image should work. The completed collage was re-photographed and a print made on resin-coated photographic paper ready for hand tinting.

This stage of the work employs much the same technique as have been described in earlier chapters of the book, but obviously the emphasis is on transparent colours so that the photographic detail remains dominant. For the most part, bottled watercolours have been used, since they work well with photographic paper, but gouache can also be tried if part of the image needs to be obscured. There are also special photographic dyes available for hand tinting prints, but you can try anything if it produces the image you want.

The second example, 'Flying Cups and Saucers', is slightly different from the first in that the composite parts – three separate cup and saucer shots, plus the landscape shot, are printed on photographic paper to retain the full tonal range of the images.

More care, and a very sharp blade, is needed to cut through the emulsion and backing paper accurately. Indeed, some people only cut through the emulsion and carefully peel this from the backing paper so that upon re-photographing no hard shadows are cast onto the background by the paper's thickness. Experiment and experience are the key factors involved here, and a few trial runs on discarded prints are well worth the effort. If necessary, the white edges of cut-out sections of print can be toned down with paintbrush and ink before being carefully fixed in place on the final composition with spray glue. Any hand-applied tonal work you may add can be done on the montage before it is re-shot.

In 'Flying Cups and Saucers' the applied colours are bottled watercolours, although some gouache has been used in the sky to obscure unwanted detail with a rich, flatter tone. Both fixed and loose masking have been used, with freehand airbrushing, or paintbrushed colour helping to add final touches to details.

LEFT TO RIGHT: Industry Year *and* Flying Cups and Saucers, *Simon Fell*.

OTHER APPLICATIONS

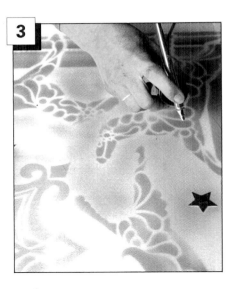

1 *Complex stencils, used in the airbrushing of fabrics, are methodically designed and carefully cut out. They are placed onto the stretched material and held in place with lead weights.*

2 *Light coats of colour are built up and frequent checks made on the density of tone achieved.*

3 *Backgrounds can be added freehand, or using simple masking procedures. Here, a tone is being applied around a star-shaped mask held down with a small lead weight.*

By using a methodical approach, this book will have instilled within you enough technical knowledge to help you understand the workings and nature of your airbrush. While the emphasis so far has been upon using it in the two-dimensional fields of illustration and retouching, it is hoped that every aspect of manipulating and controlling this versatile tool has been covered. If you now wish to use the airbrush in a field that has not been covered, you will at least have enough knowledge to solve many difficulties that might arise.

A few of the more common applications other than two-dimensional work are described in this chapter. Beyond these, there are endless uses to which the airbrush can be put, perhaps many that have yet to be thought of.

T/E/X/T/I/L/E/S

Textile design is a wonderful area for airbrush work. The light, airy freehand or stencilled designs that can be applied to scarves, tee shirts, dresses, and fabrics for all kinds of clothing or furnishing seem totally compatible with the flowing nature of the materials themselves.

Almost any textile can be sprayed with one of a number of liquid dyes which are available for airbrush use, or with correctly thinned textile printing inks. Craft shops are the most likely stockists of such materials, and they will no doubt prove to be a good source of information regarding the compatibility of various inks and dyes with different fabrics. They will also know about fixing the designs to make them washable later. Usually, though, this is done by either ironing the wrong side of the fabric or by steaming it.

Having chosen your materials you must contemplate the style of work you would prefer. A pictorial or repeat pattern type of work will doubtless require the use of stencils to spray through, while other patterns may be suited to freehand techniques. Whatever you do, you

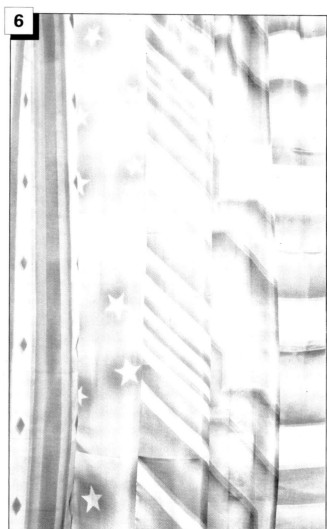

4 *The mask is removed to check for colour density.*

5 *The finished pattern is revealed.*

6 *A range of fabrics, designed and executed by Eleanor Allitt using fabric dyes on silk. When the spraying is complete, the fabric is hung and allowed to dry, which avoids creasing. The patterns are then fixed, either by ironing or steaming, depending on the type of dye used.*

should practice first of all on some off-cuts of fabric, to get used to its absorbancy and to find a method of building up colour strengths without flooding or soaking the fabric.

Stencils can be cut from special card which is available from craft shops. Simple design shapes are advised at first before you move on to complex stencils and colour interplays. It should be emphasized that white fabrics are the best to work on since then the colours you get are those you spray; there is no risk of their being dulled by the colour of the fabric itself.

To prepare your fabric for spraying, pull it flat over a large board. This can be padded with felt or other materials to create a smooth surface. Ready-made clothes, such as tee shirts, will obviously need to be arranged so that they are not unduly stretched. There should be a board inside them to prevent seepage through to the other side of the garment.

C / E / R / A / M / I / C / S

Individual and very stunning designs can be airbrushed onto pieces of ceramic that have been bisque fired. Experimentation is once more the key to achieving your own style, but various types of masking can be used including masking tape, press-down graphic lining tape and liquid masking fluid as well as various loose masks.

The medium to use is a watered-down opaque underglaze, which should be tested in your airbrush to check that it flows freely. If coarse vignettes and simple airbrushed gradations are adequate, then it will not be necessary to risk one of the more expensive double-action airbrushes for this work. As with all work, particularly if it is experimental, great care should be taken at all times with the equipment, and a face mask should be worn if pigments and media are toxic. When you have finished your design, all masking should be removed, and the resulting piece fired as normal.

ABOVE: *Special effects designer Lyle Conway is shown using the airbrush to add subtle translucent skin tones to the foam rubber model in preparation for its use in an animated film sequence.*

M/O/D/E/L/M/A/K/I/N/G

For the hobbyist who patiently assembles a detailed scale replica of a train, boat, plane or whatever, it is heartbreaking if the paint finish does not live up to the standards of craftsmanship in the model-making itself. This can often be the case if enamel or other paints are applied with a paint brush.

By using an airbrush to add, say, a mottled camouflage finish to an aircraft, or smoke stains to a steam train, or rosy cheeks to a doll's face, a more realistic painted effect can be obtained. Also, this method of painting will not clog or obscure fine details such as panel lines, and it will achieve a true-to-life finish for most mechanical subjects, since their real life counterparts are factory spray-painted.

You can use any airbrush when working on models, provided you take care. However, as it is unlikely that you will need to work with expensive double-action airbrushes, it is probably better to settle for a mid-range model. Hobby stores or modelmaking shops usually have a good selection of airbrushes, compressors and all the necessary spare parts.

The paints to use are up to you, although for plastic, clay, metals, etc, enamel paints are considered best. As with all other media they should be mixed to the consistency of milk by adding thinners, and

RIGHT: *The success of the finished model lies in the fact that the representation is believable, even though it is of an obviously fictional nature.*

ABOVE: *Mottled camouflage paint schemes, applied with spray guns to their life-size counterparts, are reproduced with an airbrush for an effective model.*

should be thoroughly flushed through the airbrush afterward. A face mask is essential when these paints and solvents are being used.

Masking can be done using various widths of masking tape, and fine lining tape for very thin lines. Large areas can be covered with scrap paper that is taped to the edge of the area to be sprayed. You will find that many of the masking techniques used by illustrators will come in handy for various forms of camouflage, such as loose masking with carefully torn paper. 'Weathering', such as smoke stains, oil marks or mud-spattered windscreens on rally cars can be achieved by experimenting with various low air pressures that give coarser grained sprays. Windscreen wiper paths, carefully traced and masked, look very effective when the masking has been removed from a mud-spattered car.

When you have completed your airbrushed special effects, you can show the model off to its best advantage on an equally realistic diorama, which will also benefit from careful airbrush work.

ABOVE: *Airbrushed murals and extravagant lettering and logos are still popular additions to customized cars and have led to a surge of interest in airbrushing generally. Special paints and lacquers can be purchased for application to car and motorbike bodies.*

C/U/S/T/O/M/I/Z/I/N/G C/A/R/S

In the late 1970s a trend among custom car owners reached its peak as a proliferation of airbrushed decorations, on every conceivable body panel, appeared on some of the most amazing automobiles ever seen. A car was often given a title or name, and the 'theme' evoked by this would be illustrated by the paint job as well as by any mechanical alterations to the body shape. Clever typography, often as not inspired by the many wonderful album cover designs of the time, would be interwoven with the illustrations and trick paint jobs to finish off the work.

Since then the cult has lost pace, or at least has shifted direction. The 1950s American cars, which were most popular at the time as subjects for custom treatment, are now sought by collectors wishing to restore them to their original state, without additional decoration. But the trend is not altogether dead, and motorbikes and trucks still make popular and handy canvases.

The process of spraying a car is much like airbrushing any other surface, although the media are different and require mastering as the cost of error is high. There are specialist books available which describe all the necessary materials and techniques used, the effects that various lacquer and enamel paints produce, as well as how to prepare and protect the finished painting. Reference to these will help you with the technical side of the art, but if you apply some of the lessons from this book you will have the best of both worlds.

F/A/S/H/I/O/N I/L/L/U/S/T/R/A/T/I/O/N

Because of the relative newness of airbrushing, very little airbrush art is what one could call 'expressive' in nature. Developments have been mainly toward improving control over the equipment used and perfecting masking techniques. This has taken airbrush art to incredible heights of realism and surrealism. But sadly it has tended to do so at the expense of artistic expression.

However, rules are made to be broken, and there are fields in which the airbrush can be used, either in a traditional controlled manner or in a looser, more personal way. One area that can make use of the whole spectrum of airbrush applications is fashion illustration.

This is a very old form of illustration, and certainly today it covers a wide field from designers' sketches, through to magazine illustration and advertising of the finished products. It is at the concept end of the fashion business, though, that there is an outlet for the expressive possibilities of the airbrush. It provides young clothes' designers with a means of applying bright colours in a variety of textures and qualities that can match the bold way that they like to express their ideas. Simple masks can be used to provide areas of colour to fabrics already drawn in with pens, pencils or markers. Or, alternatively, simple airbrush techniques on paper can suggest the shimmer or sheen of a particular material, whether it be leather or silk, plastic or wool.

FAR LEFT: *This Lee jeans poster by Bob Murdoch uses the airbrush to provide a strong graphic image, with a 1950s feel to it.*

LEFT: *Strong diagonal background stripes, created with the use of a spatter cap, work to set off this stylized fashion drawing by Simon Critchley. It is reminiscent of 1930s and 1940s advertising.*

BELOW: *A George Petty illustration for a Jantzen swimwear advertisement shows the strong style that made him one of America's topmost illustrators of the 1930s and 1940s.*

BELOW: *This individual fashion illustration by Conny Jude is produced by airbrushed flat tones and minimal vignettes.*

B/U/I/L/D/I/N/G U/P A P/O/R/T/F/O/L/I/O

If you see yourself making a living with your airbrush you will need to put together a representative portfolio of work to be seen by prospective clients or agents. Your portfolio is of the utmost importance and will remain so throughout your career. Finding the correct range of work for that portfolio is not an easy job. You must identify clearly the area of work that you are best suited to. Having done this, cover as much ground as possible within that area to present a comprehensive selection of illustrations that display all of your abilities. You may even have to be prepared to subtly change the emphasis of your portfolio to appease the whims of different clients in order to convince them of your suitability to supply the work they need.

All of this can take a considerable time to achieve. Certainly, the easiest way to lay the foundations of a career in illustration of any kind is to have an art education. This provides general background knowledge and also encourages and develops whatever skills and abilities you possess. It also gives you the time and means to identify the area of work which suits you best. Furthermore, a thorough art education will see to it that you possess more than just an ability with an airbrush.

The aims of the portfolio are to emphasize your technical strengths and versatility, and generally to show off a strong, usable, individual illustrative style. This will mean preparing examples of work covering various subjects, but avoid the trap of suggesting that you are a jack-of-all-trades, master-of-none type of illustrator. Remember to preserve a unifying notion of yourself when planning work for your portfolio – aim to tax yourself technically without breaking the boundaries of your chosen area. Consider the requirements of prospective clients within that area, and make their job easier by producing pieces of work that they can identify with. It is a pointless exercise to try and convince an art director that you could do the cutaway illustration of the oil rig required while displaying some of your own esoteric meanderings more suited to fantasy literature!

The number of pieces of work you put into a portfolio is up to you, but a few brilliant pieces on their own will make a far better impression than those same few pieces padded out with some second-rate items. After all, showing anything other than your best only proves that you are fallible and possibly even inconsistent.

Of course, the first job is always the hardest to find. If your work sparkles, and has strength, immediacy and artistic flair, people will be only too happy to give you work. On the other hand, if you are offering something either too new and different, or something competent but not necessarily better than what is around already, you can run into the famous catch where art directors like to see work that has been printed, and tell you to come back when you have had something published somewhere. So to get published you have to have been published – a vicious circle!

There are ways around that problem. The first is by the sheer physical endeavour of hauling your work around and knocking on as many doors as possible, often several times on the same door, just to remind people of your existence. Just being in the right place at the right time could gain you the first commission. Generally, a more sensible solution is to get an agent. Again this can mean trying quite a few before you have any luck, but once you have an agent you have somebody who will do all the foot-work and knock on all the right doors for you.

LEFT: *This strikingly impressive illustration by Mick Hill would make an ideal technical portfolio piece.*

D/I/S/P/L/A/Y/I/N/G P/O/R/T/F/O/L/I/O

Having established the importance of your portfolio, it is sensible to stop and consider how you should present it to its best advantage.

There are many makes and styles of artwork portfolios around, but by far the best for the illustrator are the ones containing clear plastic sleeves into which each piece of artwork can be slid for display. These protect the work from accidents and handling, while also organizing, neatly and orderly, the fruits of your labours.

There are various sizes available and initially the limiting factor will be the size of your artwork. Many people start with a large portfolio before realizing that they are cumbersome and heavy things to carry around. However, if you want to haul your valuable originals around it may be a necessity. As an alternative, it is worth considering carrying only photographic prints of your work. The advantage of prints are that they are lighter, usually smaller, and infinitely less valuable than originals. Admittedly, it is expensive to have all your work photographed and printed professionally when just starting, but it will prove worthwhile in the long run. As you progress and your work sees print, you will be able to get specimens from your clients to add to the portfolio and you can leave your originals safely at home.

In laying out the portfolio the best rule is to avoid clutter, and keep to as few images at each turn of a sleeve as possible. Keep everything clean and simple, and try to fit all the images the same way up so that you avoid having to turn the portfolio around while describing or talking about the contents. Have extra sleeves available for different categories of work so that you can change the emphasis of the portfolio for different clients.

AMERICAN FOOTBALLER

by Brett Breckon

This example was undertaken as a portfolio piece to demonstrate the possibilities of spatter cap illustration. The whole image was painted in gouache on a black background, using loose masks throughout.

APPENDIX

G/L/O/S/S/A/R/Y

Acetate A transparent film available in a variety of thicknesses which can be used as a surface in animation; for overlays; or cut into different shapes for stencils.

Airbrush Invented by the watercolour artist Charles Burdick in 1893, the airbrush is a mechanical colouring tool which mixes air and paint together and propels the combination at a surface in the form of a fine spray. The airbrush consists of a fine internal needle, a nozzle where air and paint are mixed, a colour receptacle and a pen-shaped body. It is connected by a hose to a propelling device and operated by a lever or push-button control. *(See Double-action independent; Double-action fixed; External mix; Internal mix; Single-action fixed.)*

Air eraser A device operating on the same principle as an airbrush, the air eraser is used to propel fine particles of an abrasive, thus removing unwanted areas or mistakes from artwork. It is more subtle in its effect than ordinary methods of erasing.

Air pump A component of a compressor which compresses air and forces it into the hose and thence to the airbrush.

Air trap *See Moisture trap.*

Brushwork Many airbrushed illustrations include a fair proportion of brushwork, hand-painted work with a hair paintbrush. Brushwork is usually the final stage of an airbrush painting and is often restricted to fine detail or special textured effects, such as stippling.

Cam A mechanism incorporated in some designs of double-action independent airbrushes, by which the needle is preset in one position for constant spraying.

Colour cup or jar Receptacle for holding a quantity of medium which is either mounted on the side, recessed into the top or attached to the underside of the airbrush. In the latter case, the receptacle is often in the form of a detachable jar.

Compressor The usual propellant used to power airbrushes, the compressor has a motor which maintains an air supply at a certain pressure. There are two main types: storage and direct compressors.

Containerized air A form of air supply, aside from compressors, provided by car tyres, air cans, and carbon dioxide cylinders.

Cutaway A style of technical illustration in which the internal components of a complicated mechanism, for example, a car engine, are revealed by cutting away a portion of the outer casing. This usually involves careful study of existing technical drawings; in some cases, the mechanism may actually be cut to provide reference. As is the convention, the cut sections are shown in red in the finished illustration.

Direct compressor A small compressor which does not have a reservoir tank for the air. The air supply is created by a motor fitted with a diaphragm system and pumped directly to the hose connected with the airbrush.

Double-action fixed A type of airbrush design in which the lever controls the supply of paint and air. The paint-air ratio cannot be varied.

Double-action independent The most versatile airbrush design, in which the lever controls the proportion of paint to air and the artist can regulate the density of the spray.

External mix The simplest type of airbrush design, in which the air and paint are combined outside the body of the airbrush. Most spray guns are of this type.

Fixed film masking Transparent film with a low-tack adhesive backing is the most popular material for hard-edge masking.

Freehand Freehand spraying is using the airbrush without masking of any kind.

Ghosting A highly skilled technique of representing the internal workings of a mechanism in technical illustration. The ghosted image – or phantom view – is produced by making the surface layer seem transparent, as if looking through the outside.

Gravity feed A method of supplying the medium in which the fluid reservoir is mounted above or to one side of the air channel and gravity draws the paint into the brush.

Ground The ground is the material to which the paint is applied, be it paper, art board, acetate and so on.

Gum arabic A soluble gum which is obtained from the acacia plant. It is traditionally used as a binding agent in watercolours, gouache and pastel. Gum arabic solution (one part gum arabic to two parts water) is sprayed through the airbrush to fix a layer of gouache paint.

Hard-edged The type of airbrushing which displays clean, sharp edges and is produced by masking film – or hard masking.

Hard masking In general, masking which adheres to the surface, giving sharp outlines.

Highlights The lightest areas of an illustration. They can be created by spraying white, if an opaque medium is used, or by leaving areas masked until the last stage if a transparent medium is used. Highlights can also be scratched back or rubbed back with a hard rubber.

Hose Connects the airbrush to the air supply.

Hot Pressed paper Also known as H.P. paper, it has an extremely smooth surface, ideal for precise airbrush work.

Internal mix Most airbrushes are designed so that the air and paint are combined within the nozzle to give a fine even spray.

Isometric projection A pictorial projection used in producing a three-dimensional representation of an object when all three faces are equally inclined to the plane of the projection. All the edges are foreshortened equally.

Keyline illustration A form of technical illustration where a keyline is superimposed onto a painted image to define and emphasize details and the underlying structure.

Liquid mask A rubber compound solution which can be painted onto a surface and dries to act as a mask. It can be peeled or rubbed away when the airbrushing is finished.

Loose masking Any mask which is not stuck down to the surface.

Mask A mask is simply anything which prevents the spray from reaching the surface. *(See Fixed film masking; Hard masking; Liquid mask; Loose masking; Soft masking; Stencil.)*

Medium In theory, almost anything which can be made to a certain liquid consistency can be blown through an airbrush. In practice, the most useful media are watercolour, ink and gouache.

Modelling The way artists build up the representation of three-dimensional forms on a flat surface to give the impression of volume and depth.

Moisture trap A unit which fits between the compressor and the airbrush to remove water from the air. Without a moisture trap, condensation can build up and cause blotting or uneven paint flow.

Montage Method of combining parts of different images – often photographs – to make a new composition.

Mouth diffuser A very simple form of spraying tool. Two hollow tubes are hinged together at right angles. Air is blown through the upper, horizontal tube and causes paint to be drawn in the vertical tube which is placed in a jar of paint. The paint mixes with the air, making a spray.

Needle One of the most important and delicate components of the airbrush, the adjustable fluid needle controls the flow of medium.

Nozzle The tapered casing which contains the needle and in which the air and paint supplies are combined.

'O' ring Tiny circular rubber washer at the base of the nozzle, present in many airbrush designs.

Opacity The power of a pigment to cover or obscure the surface to which it is applied.

Profile Illustration A style of technical illustration that details the side view or 'profile' of an object.

Regulator Attachment fitted to a compressor to allow adjustment of air pressure. It also acts as a moisture trap.

Rendering The process of working up an illustration.

Reservoir Sealed steel chamber capable of withstanding high pressure which is present in some compressors. The reservoir is fed from the air pump and supplies the airbrush with air. 'Reservoir' is also a term for the colour cup or paint well of an airbrush.

Retouching The adjustment of photographic images. The chief aims of retouching are to clean, mend, tint or edit the existing image and the airbrush is an important tool in such work.

Single-action fixed Airbrush design in which the speed or texture of the paint flow cannot be varied.

Soft-edged The type of airbrushed effect associated with the use of loose masking, where spray is allowed to drift and outlines are not clearly defined.

Soft masking Generally, masking which is not applied directly to the surface.

Spatter Granular texture effect caused by increasing the amount of paint and decreasing the amount of air.

Spatter cap Device fitted to the airbrush, replacing the nozzle cap, which gives a spattered spray.

Spray The fine mist of paint and air propelled from the airbrush at a surface. Blown-under spray can occur at the edge of a mask and may be exploited to diffuse contours. Overspray is where fine particles of paint drift over other sprayed areas.

Spray gun Heavy-duty spraying tool, capable of holding large quantities of paint.

Starburst highlight Star-shaped highlight useful for suggesting a high sheen.

Stencil Ready-made cut-out shape or template which can be used as a mask.

Storage compressor Large mechanism for supplying air, usually fitted with a moisture trap and containing a reservoir to maintain air pressure.

Suction feed In this method of supplying medium, the colour cup or receptacle is fitted underneath the fluid channel and liquid is drawn up into the path of the air. High pressure above forces a drop in pressure below, pulling the liquid up.

Technical illustration Highly finished illustration, usually of mechanical objects or systems, in which the purpose is to faithfully describe internal components, surface appearance, or both.

Torn paper mask Any piece of paper which is torn rather than cut and used as a mask. The uneven nature of such tears gives an effect which is useful for suggesting reflections.

Turbo airbrush The most precise type of airbrush available, the turbo is also the most complex to master, and is therefore not recommended for the novice.

Vignette An area of graduated tone, either within a shape or extended to create a background.

U/S/E M/E/D/I/A A/N/D S/U/I/T/A/B/I/L/I/T/Y

☛ SUITABLE FOR THIS TYPE OF WORK

	Photo retouching	General illustration	Large backgrounds	Model making	Car customizing	Fine art painting	Fabric painting
Badger 350-F				☛	☛	☛	☛
Badger 350-M			Up to A3	☛	☛	Large areas only	☛
Badger 350-H			Up to A2	☛	☛	Large areas only	☛
Badger 200 EX		Flat colours only	☛	☛	☛	☛	☛
Badger 100 GXF	☛	☛					
Badger 100 XF	☛	☛					
Badger 100 IL		☛					
Badger 100 LGXF	☛	☛					
Badger 100 LGIL		☛		☛		☛	
Badger 100 LGHD		☛	☛	☛	☛	☛	☛
Badger 150 XF	☛	☛					
Badger 150 IL		☛		☛		☛	
Badger 150 HD		☛	☛	☛	☛	☛	☛
Badger 400 Touch-up Gun			☛	Large scale only	☛	☛	☛
Conopois	☛	☛					
De Vilbiss Super 63A	☛	☛		Only small items			
De Vilbiss Super 63E	☛	☛	Up to A3	☛	☛	☛	☛
De Vilbiss Sprite		☛	Up to A3	☛	☛	☛	☛
De Vilbiss Sprite Major			Up to A2	☛	☛	Large areas only	☛
De Vilbiss MP C-C		☛	☛	☛	☛	☛	☛
De Vilbiss MP 1-1			☛	Large scale only	☛	☛	☛
De Vilbiss MP 2-2			☛	Large scale only	☛	☛	☛
De Vilbiss MP 3-3			☛	Large scale only	☛	☛	☛
Hohmi Y3		☛	☛	☛		☛	☛
Iwata HP-A	☛	☛					
Iwata HP-B	☛	☛					
Iwata HP-C	☛	☛		☛		☛	☛
Iwata E-1		☛	☛	☛			
Iwata E-2		☛	☛	☛	☛	☛	
Iwata SB		☛		☛	☛	☛	☛
Iwata BC		☛	☛	☛	☛	☛	☛
Iwata BE-1		☛	☛	☛	☛	☛	☛
Iwata BE-2		☛	☛	☛	☛	☛	☛
Olympos HP-100A	☛	☛					
Olympos HP-100B	☛	☛		☛			
Olympos HP-100C		☛		☛		☛	
Olympos SP-A	☛	☛					
Olympos SP-B	☛	☛		☛			
Olympos SP-C		☛		☛		☛	
Paasche F-1				☛			
Paasche H-1				☛	☛	☛	☛
Paasche H-3			Up to A3	☛	☛	☛	☛
Paasche H-5			Up to A2	☛	☛	☛	☛
Paasche VJR	☛	☛					
Paasche V-1	☛	☛					
Paasche VLS-1		☛		☛		☛	☛
Paasche VLS-3		☛		☛	☛	☛	☛
Paasche VLS-5		☛	☛	☛	☛	☛	☛
Paasche AB Turbo	☛	☛					
Rich AB-100	☛	☛					
Rich AB-200	☛	☛					
Rich AB-300		☛		☛		☛	
Thayer & Chandler Model A		☛	☛				
Thayer & Chandler Model AA	☛	☛					
Thayer & Chandler Model C		☛	☛	☛	☛	☛	☛
Thayer & Chandler Model E		☛	☛	☛	☛	☛	☛
Thayer & Chandler Model G		☛	☛	☛	☛	☛	☛

U S E

The airbrushes on sale at present cater for every need, from detail spraying of small areas to painting large expanses. If you have a specific requirement, such as model making, you can buy an airbrush tailored to your own needs, which will take the right medium you require. However, if your airbrushing is more varied in nature, there are several general-purpose airbrushes which can be used in a variety of situations with a large range of media. Pick the most suitable airbrushes from the chart and then ask to try them out in the shop to see if they have the indefinable quality of 'feel' which suits you.

Artists' watercolours	Gouache	Acrylic colours	Artists' oil colours	Modelmakers' enamels	Cellulose paint	Fabric colours	Waterproof inks
►	►			►		►	
Large areas	Medium areas			►	With extreme care	►	Large areas
Large areas	Medium area			►	With extreme care	►	Large areas
►	►	►	►	►	►	►	►
►	►						►
►	►						►
►	►						►
►	►						►
►	►			►			►
►	►	►	►	►	►	►	►
►	►						►
►	►			►			►
►	►	►	►	►	►	►	►
►	►	►	►	►	►	►	►
►	►						With care
►	►	With care					►
►	►	►	►	►	With care	►	►
►	►	►	►	►	►	►	►
►	►	►	►	►	►	►	►
►	►	►	►	►	►	►	►
►	►	►	►	►	►	►	►
►	►	►	►	►	►	►	►
►	With care						With care
►	►						►
►	►	With care	With care	With care			►
►	►	►	►	►	►	►	►
►	►	►	►	►	►	►	►
►	With care	►	►	►	►	►	►
►	With care	►	►	►	►	►	►
►	►	►	►	►	►	►	►
►	With care						With care
►	►						With care
►	►	With care	With care				►
►	With care						With care
►	►						With care
►	►	With care	With care				►
►	►			►			►
►	►			►			►
►	►			►	With care	►	►
►	►			►	With care	►	Large areas
►	►			►	With care	►	Large areas
►	►						►
►	►						►
►	►	►	►	►		►	►
►	►	►	►	►		►	►
►	►	►	►	►	►	►	►
►							►
►	With care						With care
►	►						►
►	►	►	►	►		►	►
►	With care						With care
►	With care						►
►	►	►	►	►	►	►	►
►	►	►	►	►	►	►	►
►	►	►	►	►	►	►	►

MEDIA

I/N/D/E/X

P/I/C/T/U/R/E C/R/E/D/I/T/S

Key: *t* = top, *b* = bottom, *l* = left, *r* = right.

The author and publishers have made every effort to identify the copyright owners of the pictures; they apologize for any omissions and would like to acknowledge the following:–

Eleanor Allitt: pp 108, 109. Melvyn Bagshaw: pp 55–59, 74–80. Clive Boden: pp 10/11, 22, 25, 28, 38. Brett Breckon: pp 6, 7, 18, 20, 21, 39, 40, 41, 60, 63, 68 *b*, 69, 71, 73, 81, 82, 89, 91 *b*, 98–101, 119. Colour Library Int: p 113. Lyle Conway: pp 110, 111. Gordon Cramp Studios: pp 95 *t*, 97. DeVilbiss Ltd: p 112. Falmouth School of Art and Design: pp 64, 114 *r* (Simon Critchley); p 70 (Paul Wood); pp 84/85 (Paul Davie); pp 90, 91 *t* (Alan Holwill); p 88 (Mark Healey); p 103. Simon Fell: pp 104/105. Fisher Fine Art: pp 30. Folio/Ean Taylor: pp 23, 72. Mick Hill: pp 61, 62, 116/117. Hipgnosis: p 95 *b*. Ian Howes: pp 32, 33, 42, 68 *t*. Imperial War Museum, London: p 29. Jantzen Inc: p 115 *r*. Conny Jude: p 115 *l*. Richard Manning: p 24. Brent Moore: pp 14/15, 16, Chris Moore: p 31. Bob Murdoch: p 114 *l*. Rolls Royce Ltd: p 86. John Shipston: p 102. Joan Honour Smith/Warner Bros: pp 94, 96. Roger Stewart: p 34. West Glamorgan Institute of Higher Education: pp 26, 27, 65, 67 (Lloyd Bugler); p 51 (Andy Penaluna).